To Chri...
Be stil —
what does your heart
Tell you?

Jump on the Love Train
Many hearts await you

Much love to you

Rae Lewis

By Rae Lewis

RaeLewis@sonomic.net

outskirts
press

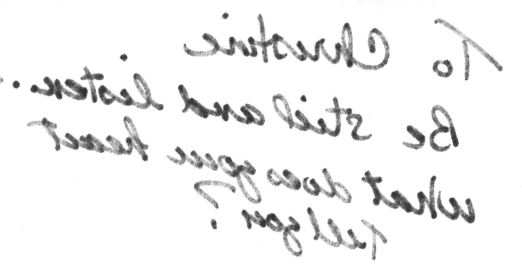

Declaration

Most names and stories are a creative blend of events so that identifying details have been changed in order to protect the privacy of those who have been in contact with Chicuchas Wasi over the years, unless they have agreed to be included by testimony, photo and/or name in this history.

We are unable to include the many beautiful photos of the children of our 31 years and the school girls who live in rural Andean Peru. You are welcome to visit us on www.chicuchaswasi.org or on FaceBook: chicuchaswasi to learn much more than this book is able to cover.

Dedication

To all the children who grew up in the CW Shelter filling the house with love and laughter and to the current students and alumnae girls of the CW School for girls who keep the love flowing each and every day along with the CW teachers and staff; to our supporters at large, who all together comprise the CW extended family, we extend our sincerest gratitude and appreciation.

Table of Contents

Introduction

Many people have asked what inspired me to create Chicuchas Wasi (The Children's Project), a lone woman of 41, new to Cusco, Peru and with no Spanish, in 1986. The truth was I was terrified, yet I found the courage to do it anyway. I was strong in character but could quickly become weak-kneed. In a leap of faith, I stepped alone into the unknown, both extremely exciting and a bit scary.

Religion was not a part of my family life. I explored different churches on my own growing up, but felt no attachment to them, although I did feel a soft calling from deep inside me. In my heart I knew I was never alone. And I trusted that knowing. Since my thirties, I have felt a growing presence and the subtle guidance of Divine Mother, gently pushing me to get on the train She is driving.

With that said, I believe one person can be the spark to jumpstart others for the greater good. In the 31 years since the Chicuchas Wasi Shelter, and later The School for Forgotten Girls was founded, I now recognize who I am – "that spark."

Born at the end of WWII to eccentric and adventurous parents and because of their unusual and courageous examples and unconventional lifestyle, I was given permission to step out of the box, feel freedom and learn to fly.

Our cookie-cutter house backed up dangerously to the railroad tracks in Tiburon and didn't protect little kids like me from putting pennies on the railroad track, delighted to watch the train smash them flat or prevent us from climbing on top of the tunnel to shake, rattle and roll as the old train vibrated through underneath.

While attending primary school in Marin, my dad sold our house to buy an old 45-foot wood hull boat from the shipyard. He and my boat-builder grandfather caulked the decks and built the boathouse to make it ready to begin his new sport fishing business. With no brothers and the eldest of two girls in the family, I was chosen to work the sport-fishing trips, the only 12-year-old girl non-union deckhand I ever met. Every weekend and all summer we were up at 4:00 a.m., picked up our fishermen and their bait and sinkers at the Sausalito Bait & Tackle Shop pier, boarded the 'Bluefin' and steamed out under the Golden Gate Bridge towards the Farallon Islands with the rest of the fishing fleet to catch salmon. When the men had the bait and sinkers on their line and had thrown the line in the water to wait for their catch, my work was temporarily done. My favorite place on the boat was the bow, lying by the anchor chain for hours. I would lose my teenage self in the dark green water we earlier sliced through, now a glistening mystery of bright shafts of sunlight stabbing deep into oblivion, like a light trance with an occasional giant jellyfish pumping by. It felt wonderful and otherworldly. As a girl, I liked that I lived outside the lines of normal, developed a bit of gypsy spirit and enjoyed the taste of freedom the sea gave me. I developed a yearning deep inside I thought everyone had and knew there was more to come.

As a family we moved a lot from apartment to apartment, one adventure after another to be near our boat, the Bluefin, berthed in Sausalito. Our one-bedroom Sausalito apartment was modest, but enough for the bunkbed I shared with Chris, my younger sister, while Mom and Dad slept on the sofa bed in the living room. In such a small apartment the late-night conversations of my parents were easy to hear, and it was no surprise when we soon had the larger 65-foot 'Blue Spirit' and a much bigger adventure. My parents decided we could live on the bigger boat in the harbor to save money until they were ready to try their hand at commercial fishing. The head (toilet) was not set up yet so we had the dreaded bucket with a rope on it for our toilet, before the bay rules forbade dumping sewage in the bay. A round galvanized cattle water trough was our bathtub in the galley, and we heated one inch of water on the kerosene stove to bathe, my sister and I sharing the water after a knock-down battle on who would go first. Whenever I invited a friend to spend the night on the boat their parents always ended up inviting me to their home instead. They had a real shower with hot and cold water and that was perfect for me.

Chris hated our living situation and followed my lead with sleepovers at her friend's home too.

Below deck my sister and I shared a stateroom next to the engine room. My dad placed each mattress on top of a bunch of oil drums with sheets and an electric blanket covered in plastic, in case of a deck leak in the rain. The icebox at the foot of my bed almost daily needed a big block of ice and made a wet mess if we forgot. The best sleep I ever had was in this bed from being rocked to sleep with the gentle motion of the water and listening to the soft splashes against the outer hull of our bedroom. Chris was four years younger and very opinionated about living on the boat and was not impressed with this adventure like I was. My main frustration was that I lost many of my paperbacks as they fell between the outer and inner hull I used as a bookshelf next to my bed. Sadly, the space between the two hulls ate my books.

A strong swimmer, my next job was to check the propeller for any ropes tangled around it. I learned to keep my mouth shut and only open my eyes when I had to. Suffice to say, I became resilient at a very young age. The family boating business later morphed into Tourism to take tourists on the 'Cruise with Lewis SF Bay Tour' and my family responsibility changed. Now, I had to dress up to look 18 and do the family business PR at the San Francisco hotels, and I was off to sell our tours to the hotel tourists. My sister spent most days in our SF Fisherman's Wharf's tiny ticket office at Pier 43 next to Grotto #9 and hiding inside behind the window while Mom donned a black and white jail suit and megaphone to bark trips to Alcatraz. My girlfriends, Sue and Dolly, (who worked for my family) fanned out with a fist full of brochures to entice the tourists.

Not unusual for a woman born in the WWII era, I married while still a teen and was blessed with three beautiful baby boys by age 24. The following years were dedicated to raising my very active sons and kept me busy. My days were filled with love and contentment and a lot of diapers. The boys were still very young when my husband's work took our family to Honolulu. While in Hawaii and with the boys in school I earned my Real Estate license and sold homes for four years and gave the family a financial boost.

Upon returning to the mainland and California we moved our young family to then rural Sonoma County and we purchased some acreage to build a home. All of us: Mom, Dad and the three kids, grandfather Lee and contractor uncle Dick worked together to build our new home. We put on the carpenter belt ready with hammer and other tools and pounded way too many nails into plywood on the floor and up on the roof. We drilled a well and had a septic system installed and soon moved into our new ranch style country home. Too soon we began raising cows, sheep, pigs, goats, rabbits and chickens, created an organic garden, and the boys joined 4H. All three grew up with little league baseball, soccer, football and even tennis, while I sold hot dogs during the games and ate the hot summer dust of the field. Suddenly our boys were bringing home girls for a BBQ and borrowing the car for the prom and homecoming games. The boys were in middle and high school when I entered college in my 30s. They one by one graduated along with their mother in 1979, one from primary school, and one from high school and me from college with my RN. Our oldest son went to work while he contemplated his future. My little babies had become intelligent and independent-thinking young men and it was all happening too soon. Still the younger two were in high school while I worked in several nearby hospitals in critical care. I also worked with hospice and as a Therapeutic Touch (TT) healer privately offering energy healing for patients while teaching TT to medical and private individuals in our home.

My youngest son was in his last year of high school, his brother (two years his senior) was in college, and our eldest son decided to join the Air Force. Our family life was beginning to change. When very young couples marry, they often mature into different people and that occurred in my marriage; my husband matured one way and I the opposite way. My marriage ended at 40, and my life turned upside down. Two years later, it was clear that it would stay that way — like it or not. I was re-inventing myself from a wife of 24 years and dedicated mother to three sons to life as a single woman with now independent, grown sons. I didn't know what 'THAT' looked like. The last time I knew single life was as a gun-chewing, slang-slinging, boy-crazy teen. Reverting to the single life I remembered would definitely not look good on a now 40-year-old. So, I tripped and stumbled my way for two years, until Claudia, a TT and nursing colleague, telephoned her excited offer: *I have the perfect trip for you, The Inca Trail to Machu Picchu – in Cusco. Peru – Interested?*

Growing up in my family was one big lesson in how to adapt to change and develop the capacity to rebound intact and overall one big adventure. The constant variety kept me interested and I did well with the craziness over the years. I developed an adventurous gypsy-like spirit and a curiosity to understand many things about my world and worlds I had yet to meet. I tend to live on the edge at times and take more risks than most would feel safe doing. However, I always knew I was safe and protected by a greater force. Among them was the Level 4 difficult, but incredible, 'Inca Trail Trek Machu Picchu in the Andes of Peru' with my colleague Claudia. A complete surprise to me was my reaction being in Cusco and on the Inca Trail. Strong confusing emotions made me a blubbering basket case with a strong sense of connection to Peru, which I didn't understand. Peru was not on my radar, nor did I ever imagine Peru would call to me. To learn the rest of this story you will have to read the pages that follow.

CHAPTER 1

Inca Trail Trek — 1985

*"You were born with wings,
why prefer to crawl through life?"* — Rumi

RING-RING-RING, JUST AS I'm about to close the front door. It's Claudia, the marathon wonder woman since she came in second in the Bay to Breaker race last June. She is talking so fast I can't get a word in. *Remember when you said you wanted some meaningful travel — something special, really adventurous? Here it is — a trek to Machu Picchu with some great Sierra Club folks. It leaves in two weeks. What do you think, Rae?*

Out of breath. My mouth hangs open, unable to move. My thoughts are fighting in my head like a Scrabble destruction derby: *I can't go. I'm not a runner like she is; I'd hold everyone back. I wheeze when I run to my mailbox, for God's sake. I don't know any of the 20 Stanford Alumnae going. She wants to embarrass me, show me how good she is. I've never trekked in my life nor owned real hiking boots or a backpack. If it wasn't a grade 4 trek, It would be everything I want...But...It's 13,000 feet up there. Impossible! I'll get altitude sickness.*

"I'll call you tonight," I told her, hanging up and running out the door to work. I can't be late again. As an RN in the GYN department

at the medical center, I have a new group to prepare today for the infertility program.

Between patients, the energy around Claudia and I hiking side-by-side to Machu Picchu intensifies as my great adventure trip spreads like a wildfire throughout the clinic. By the end of the day, my colleagues handed me a revised schedule with their names in place of mine for the two weeks I will be gone. I am covered to go. Didn't they hear me say I am not prepared to do a trek like this? They're medical people and know the risks of a hike like this in high altitude when the person is not physically fit. When I whine that I really can't go, they respond: *"How can you NOT go? And if you do have any trouble, Claudia has done this a million times and will be there. What an opportunity!"* They tell me I am just afraid, and they are right; I am. If I get sick, I won't be alone. Claudia will be my tent mate, and she is an RN with experience. Listen to me talk myself into this. And the spell of it all grows.

For two weeks I pushed myself to exhaustion running up and down hills, my new book-filled backpack weighing heavily on my back and wearing my new boots during my lunch break. I pray I can do this and realize how badly I want to.

First Look at Cusco

"I can't see it!" I relay to Claudia, irritated that she can, my nose pressed to the glass. Looking through the tiny scratched window at the adobe-red city sprawled below, I am straining to find any feline shape. Our study book says, 'The Capitol of the Ancient Incan Empire is in the shape of a Puma,' but today I don't see any puma down there...

Our plane circles and drops between the folds of mountains exiting out over a valley, *long and shaped like the puma*, swears Claudia. Small, tile-roofed with mud-block houses line both sides of the airstrip. The wheels touch ground with only a bump bump, and we're down. From the plane I can see a petite barefoot child with a bucket collecting water from an outdoor water spigot. A man with a stick taps his cow's rear while walking down one of many unpaved red roads — in fact everything is stained the color of this red earth. The city of Cusco rests gently between majestic snow-capped mountains at 12,000 feet and is held in the arms of the Apus (Andean Gods), my guidebook says.

Our Aeroperu flight taxis around the end of the airstrip, and we are so close I can almost touch a red VW spewing black exhaust over a passing man pedaling his three-wheeled bicycle cart piled high with cabbage and green squash on a side street not 40 feet away. Our plane noses toward a small two-story gray cement building with the letters, 'Cusco International Airport' big enough for passing planes to see, and rolls to a stop. Outside two young men in street clothes push the moveable stairs up to our door. The cabin passengers are in fast forward to get their bags and packages from the overhead compartment, and squeeze into the line of impatience, for the moment going nowhere.

A burst of sunlight and brisk thin Andean air enters as the door opens. A gentle, sweet-faced native lets me into the pressed line. When my turn comes to climb down the metal stairs juggling my heavy bag, I am sure my arms are longer now, like the ape. I am breathing hard like something tight is around my chest. When my feet hit the asphalt, I turn to Claudia smiling so big my cheeks hurt, giggling, *"We are in Cusco."* She responds all smiles. Hearing a ruckus behind us, we turned and joined the whoops of joy from the rest of our group. Breathing slower and more easily now, I want to savor the high mountain crisp air, so refreshing after awful gray Lima, and helping the oxygen molecules hold tight.

The group surrounds the conveyer belt in the baggage claim area, and I slip in the middle. The laughing frequent travelers stand side-by-side the apprehensive first-timers. I am admittedly excited. No bags appear yet. Looking outside, my eyes survey the crowd of hopeful men holding up Hotel signs and shouting *"taxi"* and wildly waving arms outside every door and window. They are all blocked by a serious, mean-looking green-clad security man who won't let them inside. I find out why when we have to push out and through the crowd to our waiting bus. I am grateful our guide is blazing a trail for us. One glance at this crowd shouting Taxi, and Guide Madame and words in Spanish I don't understand, and I realize what a challenge it would be to fend off these competitive hustlers alone, who I see wanting a green piece of this pale face. They were ready to pounce; like a swarm of bees spotting sweet honey smeared all over a resting bear. I hung tight with the rest to the bus and we were off to our hotel to settle in for the night.

We received the standard welcome of Coca Tea and instructions for today to prepare for the start of our trek in the morning. We headed obediently to our assigned rooms for the obligatory nap to gently allow our bodies to ease into the high altitude and ward off symptoms of Seroche (altitude sickness). Our bags were packed for storage and the items we needed for the trek were in our backpack ready for the morning. It was not easy to fall asleep in such an exciting ancient culture like this Inca world outside of the hotel doors. Sleep was nowhere near me and I decided a little wander close to the hotel should be OK. I made it just a block away and felt as if I would be on the ground any minute and quickly returned to my room. I learned I had better follow the instructions next time. I did nap a bit in spite of the altitude headache that I now had. I recall we had a simple dinner but could taste none of it and returned for the night. I knew tomorrow would take all my energy.

The Trek Begins to Machu Picchu

Finally, the day came, and we put on our boots and backpack and headed to board the train at Kilometer 88, the beginning of our trek. We are about to walk in the footsteps of the ancient Incans to Machu Picchu on the very path they took. The group chattered about this site and an Inca King in a fight with another and about the Conquistador Pizarro. I didn't know what they were talking about because I didn't have time to read the information. For this Stanford alumnae study tour to the ancient ruins of Cusco, we were given two thick books to read: 'Conquest of the Incas by Hiram Bingham' and another I can't remember, neither one I finished. I regret only scanning the Syllabus for this trip and vow to read it tonight.

First, the Important Coca Lesson

After a short train ride from Cusco, we arrive to the village of Chillca, to find the porters and their burros already loaded with our supplies. Forty porters are hunched together cramming their cheeks with coca leaves taken from colorful, small, hand-woven pouches hung around their necks and loading our cargo onto their backs. I looked down at the latest hiking boots from REI that adorned the feet of our group of 20 and then to the strong broad feet that wore only sandals made of old tires for this trek. As I watched this enormous effort, I was not just a little embarrassed that we North Americans require so much.

Then it was our turn. We tightened our shoelaces and slid our arms through daypacks filled with water, socks, moleskin and extra shoes, trail mix from home and rainwear. Lastly, we circled closely for an almost whispered lesson in coca leaf chewing: stuff a handful of leaves into cheek pocket, chew lightly to moisten, bite small amount of black lime off the ugly clay-looking ball and masticate slightly until tongue is numb. Then you suck and spit, suck and spit, as you walk to ward off thirst, air, hunger and exhaustion. Claudia looked like a chipmunk oozing disgusting green/black slime onto her lips like old motor oil. The green-black drool I was wiping off my mouth was enough for me. I spit the bitter stuff out into the bushes alongside Claudia, noting we were the only weak-hearted in the bunch and the youngest at 41 among these hearty 70-year-old trekkers chewing and spitting happily as we began our trek.

Our first few hours on the trail were easy and relatively flat though still climbing under a gentle sun. Then it changed. My knees were acting up for the first time ever, and I felt not-myself-strange emotionally. But wanting to be a part of the group experience, I pushed through it. We began to weave and wind and leave thick brush and clusters of trees behind. Fewer and fewer places of shade were available and the weather threatened to soak us. It did rain, but lightly, on our plastic ponchos creating a sticky sauna between the poncho and our skin.

This hardy group of strangers and I arrived at our first camp that embraced us with powerful Andean mountains. The tents were already set up next to a row of potty tents off to the right of camp, each placed carefully over two-foot-deep holes dug for the occasion. We settled in to check our feet for blisters and clean up in the basin of water placed before our tent. By late day, my right knee was aching seriously, and became so uncomfortable it was hard to walk — not a good thing on a trek. I massaged it, downed an anti-inflammatory to get through the day, and that night at the camp welcomed a local healing remedy of a smelly hot liquid of unknown origin by one of the porters whose soothing massage of this stinky stuff around my knee brought relief. But something deeper was stirring inside me — something ancient remembered, touching me now. I didn't know what that was. At one point I experienced a sense of *Deja vu* so profound that I stood frozen in my boots and backpack blocking the narrow trail with chocking sobs spilling out of my mouth. It was like reuniting with long-dead loved ones. Too powerful to ignore I knew I had to learn why.

The keepers of our creature comforts are a curious lot. The few trees around were bunched together, and under them a dozen or so porters gathered to hang blue plastic sheets for protection from any night rain. They use no tents, down sleeping bags with soft mats under them or leather boots. They simply roll in a blanket and lie on the ground close together for warmth. For their evening entertainment they huddled together, smiling, laughing and watching us as if they were all watching the funniest movie ever. We were that movie.

Our first night at camp was full of laughter and jokes. Among my new and experienced trekking friends, someone had a small bottle of Pisco, and someone else had lemon-lime dry powder. Stir it all together and *Voila!* — Pisco sours. More laughter and more jokes and more Pisco sours and the evening flew into night, with the full moon big over us. As if a bell rang, we all suddenly remembered that tomorrow will be difficult, we will climb the highest and most difficult 16,000 ft. pass, and the night faded into snoring as each slipped off to his tent to sleep. But I couldn't sleep — not yet and stepped outside to see the huge moon overhead.

The full moon peeked at me from over white blankets capping the peaks and illuminated our camp. I was the only one still up, called out by the moon. She speaks to me, lifts me and gives me strength. I can make it over tomorrow's pass, and I will make it over the next one. *I will. I will.*

I spotted a large gold wildcat standing still against the mountain watching my every move — she looks and senses what I am. Then back and forth she struts in front of me 100 feet away while her eyes lock on me. I feel no fear; rather we are touching a rare gift from the 'Apus.' Her puma whiskers reach out to me, as if to tickle and tease an ancient memory inside me. The Quechua people honor their 'APUs' (mountain Gods) and power animals — messengers from God. A lone sweet 'quena' (flute) sings to the elements in the distance, and the strangely familiar sound makes me cry. The soulful prayer calls every peak and they answer back. Magic is in the air and the Gods are awake.

Early the next morning, after a hearty breakfast, we were back on the trail. This sky is SO big. Clean, clear, cloudless blue drapes itself like air over these naked peaks. Nothing but the heartiest of nature survives here. Today I noticed the oxygen tank that Carlos, our lead guide, carried and I haven't taken my eye off him since.

Already my co-trekkers are way ahead of me. My mental mantra continues — 'Breathe-in-out, breathe-in-out, breathe-in-out' — putting me in trance, while my head orders my muscles to work and feet to move. They obey, and the march continues higher and higher still, one foot in front of the other. Pools of stinging fluid scream in my socks: *"No more, no more,"* but the rub in my boots must continue a while longer. Breathe-step-breathe-step-breathe-step. *"Breathe, Rae!"* In-out-slow-deep, I beg each breath to go deep enough to last until the next one and make the pain go away. A vice is squeezing my chest. It hurts to breathe. *Make it go away,* I plead. Silent chant goes on: *Breath-in-out-in-out deep and slow. You can do it,* I tell myself. Keep going, keep going, higher, higher, step, step. But the ridge is not close. *Breathe-step-breathe-step, chew, suck, swallow, breathe.* Sucking hard on my half lemon, it's sweet fragrance bathes my nostrils; it's bitter liquid balm to my parched mouth. Don't talk; just breathe, just climb, just suck the bittersweet numbness. Focus on the ridge. *It's getting closer. Breathe-in-out-breathe-in-out-breathe-in-out.*

Our Indian porters run past us, hunched over and grunting with the weight of the barrels of water strapped to their backs. Some carry other cargo – our tents, tables and personal gear – like human burros running past us as we wheeze along. Their bodies are wet with sweat, their rubber tire sandaled feet caked with dry dirt, and their chests looking like the barrels they carry. As they run, they chew coca leaves; chew, spit and suck the slimy green wad positioned like a jawbreaker in their cheeks, the bitter-sweet juice of the coca leaf pricks every papillae with numbness and relieves their need for thirst, air and rest.

Breathe-step-breathe-step-breathe-step. No trees grow here. No homes dot the valleys. The naked peaks loom all around our party of 20. We have long since passed above the tree line and the entire group has long since passed me.

Somewhere along this stretch, the ridge is still in front but getting closer, when a hand lifts my pack off my back, and the person attached to that arm is walking alongside me. The one with the oxygen! My feet touch the earth, but they don't set down or lift up. My body weighs nothing; I don't think I am breathing anymore. I don't remember anything more because it felt like I was lifted to the ridge. I blinked, and I was on top. Our whole group was cheering wildly for each other, but mostly for the lone straggler— me. I was the last to cross and I was ecstatic. We descended a few hours more and found ourselves entering our camp for the night, and the smell of dinner on the stove.

Today was arduous and wonderful, and long and uplifting. I was euphoric by the time I reached and stood on that ridge. I didn't know how I got there, but my feet did and reminded me as soon as I took the boots off. Everyone was massaging their feet, passing around moleskin, and nursing sore muscles. Tomorrow we will make it to 'Inti Punku,' the gate to the ancient ruin of the Incas: Machu Picchu. The smells of something delicious brought us all to the table. Andean quinoa soup and a carbohydrate heavy main meal of choclo (Andean corn), white rice, and juicy roasted lamb pulled from piled rocks that created an impromptu earth oven. Every plate was practically licked clean by this hungry gang. We were blessed with the best cooks I could have imagined on this wilderness trek and we ate. Our mood was jovial, but our group mind seemed to be on sleep. I don't remember getting into my sleeping bag, but I must have slept well because the next morning I was refreshed and rested. The worst was over.

At the Gate of Inti Punko

Our last day on the Inca trail was full of ups and downs of large and short steps. We climbed up and then we went down, and by the early afternoon we were standing at Inti Punko staring down at the marvel called Machu Picchu.

For a long time, the group hovered at Inti Punku (The Sun Gate), eyes fixed on the sprawling ruins below us. One solo green tree grows peacefully on the only flat piece of earth in the middle. The remains of a stone city are before us and you can almost see the busy life of the Incas 2,000 years ago. Silently we wound down the last stretch of trail to Machu Picchu in awe of the beauty and the size of it all. Not a peep out of my knee, but my feeling of *Deja vu* was even stronger and my eyes were leaking softly.

Next to the ancient ruin nestled into the side of the mountain is the Machu Picchu Hotel and our home for the next two nights. We entered the well-preserved ruin and headed straight to the hotel. We will have plenty of time to explore these stones, but first a real bathroom with a real shower and hot water to stand under and I will be sure I am in heaven.

The second most beautiful site in the world was not to be mistaken the first day off the trail. We got settled in and hit the showers. The shiny clean blue tiles went from floor to ceiling in Claudia's and my hotel bathroom, and what sat in the corner dripping water was candy to my eyes. In seconds I stripped naked and entered. The warm soft spray coming out of the showerhead spreading like warm fingers down my head, my arms and back, was the best shower ever and obliterated all other thoughts. The towel was thick and rough against my skin and the brisk soaking up of the last remnants of water was a feeling of sheer pleasure. I had forgotten the feel of clean. Yes, I am sure that was heaven!

Machu Picchu is wonderful, but for me was an anticlimax after the trail. And that is another story.

I floated down the flight of stairs and into the Machu Picchu Hotel dining room in my clean blue jeans and pale blue long sleeved-shirt. The tables were covered with white tablecloths, and the seats were cushioned and covered with a deep pink print. The table was set with china, two forks and knife and spoon and white flowers in a tiny plain white vase in the center next to the tiny white bowls of salt and pepper and another filled with yellow butterballs. The sight was beautiful, but I missed the camp tent, the fold-up stool seats, the plastic plates and single fork on a fold up metal table. I missed the look of anticipation in the eyes facing me of my trek mates. Maybe this scene was just too civilized to hold onto the magic of those precious days because something had faded.

We dined in the hotel restaurant in clean clothes and celebrated our achievement. We ranged from age 40 (Claudia and I) to 73, and we had all made it and with no injuries to speak of. We had something to celebrate, and we did. Wine glasses were held up filled with red nectar and clinking each one in turn held out by clean arms covered in fresh pack-wrinkled shirts. Laughter was loud now, or so it seemed, enclosed as it was in the small room in comparison to the wild. We had become closer over the 3½ days of the trail walking and tending each other's bruises. And the comfort of the closeness felt good.

Tomorrow we would tour the ruin itself and more the day after that. Tonight, I just wanted to relax, drink in the wine and wallow in the accomplishment of our feat surrounded by laughter with my new friends. They were still going strong when I bid them goodnight, and I am one of the younger ones present. These Sierra Club people are a hardy bunch, and to see the 73-year-old couple standing on that first peak, the first to arrive and waving at the rapidly approaching others (minus one 40-year-old still at the bottom too focused on breathing to look up to smile back) was depressing.

Back in my room alone, my thoughts returned to what had happened on the trail. With Carlos and his oxygen tank at my side, my feet moved one in front of the other while my thoughts were on nothing but breathing. A bend in the trail put the happy group on the ridge out of view briefly, and in that split second my life-saving-oxygen-ready guide stopped my rhythmic breathing with what felt like an unripe cut pear smashing up against my lips. Oblivious to anything that wasn't about moving air in and out of my lungs and stepping one foot after the other, I wasn't ready for this — nor was I interested in the amorous moves from this gentleman who kindly eased my load the last part of the trek. I wasn't really sure those were lips I felt; maybe a big fly splashed its wet body on them instead. All this tenderness was lost on me, and no doubt had the effect of a bucket of cold water on our guide.

A moment later, I stood with the rest on top of the ridge staring at the trail I had just come up and was unclear how I made the leap up. To me, I was just lifted up — never have I felt such a feeling of euphoria and closeness to otherworldly help. I had placed my hand though the ethers and from the other side a strong arm took hold, made contact, and carried me up physically, but also unlocked something unknown inside me.

Uummmm, how could a bed feel so good, I wondered, snuggling down deeper under the alpaca blankets and wrapping them tightly around me, holding in the heat and the magic of my earlier thoughts. I have been touched and moved to new awareness in the last 3½ days, and I don't understand it. I want to understand and what it means, and voice out loud, *I am ready — what am I supposed to learn here?*

I woke the next morning to Claudia saying we can go into the ruin as early as we wish, and that breakfast is at eight. I dragged myself back from the faraway place I must have been visiting and got up. Claudia had partied all night with one of the group and was grinning from ear to ear about her new conquest. We showered in turns, luxuriating in the hot water, and dressed while laughing at the antics of last night. *Did I see her climb over the table?* Claudia asked. *When did that happen?* I asked, realizing I was off in another world, very far away and must have missed it. We laughed at her adolescent-like spontaneity so unlike the professional image she usually portrays. I loved hearing about it and laughed from my belly at the thought of her standing on the table in that elegant dining room.

Our guide and lecturer for the day was Alejandro from Cusco, and he told us about the window of the three sisters, and how it communicated with the similar three windows on the other side. We learned about the magnetic field around the astrological stone on the top, and he used his bent coat hangers to show us how when first held outward together they moved open as you moved closer to the stone. We climbed the slippery cliff edge rock steps up to Huayna Picchu, and laid on the rocks on top, enjoying the tiny yellow butterflies that flew and swarmed around us — hundreds of them — and looked down over the entire site that is Machu Picchu and the mysterious looking green valleys and the 'Vilcanota' river winding around it on its way to the jungle. Machu Picchu sits literally on top of this mountain, the top shaved off so that an entire stone house city could be built there. It was discovered in 1911 by Hiram Bingham. Thankfully, the Spanish Conquistador Pizzaro missed it when he ransacked Peru on his gold quest.

Later, walking through the site and talking openly to the mature fortyish and educated Cusco guide, Alejandro, I told him about my experience on the trail, that something mystical was trying to reach me and left me hungry to know what. Would he be my guide and translator upon returning to Cusco, so I might investigate this feeling further? Watching my face as I described the unusual emotions that overcame me at strange times, like when I heard an Indian playing his flute 'quena' it was so tender and familiar it left me sobbing uncontrollably in my tent. He agreed.

Before leaving for this trip, John (assistant administrator of my Clinic) came to me with a little piece of paper with the name Ernesto written down. I looked at him questioning the paper and he explained he had traveled to Machu Pichu and hiked the Inca Trail in 1968 with his wife at the time and she had become ill with Seroche (altitude sickness) and was treated by this healer named Ernesto. He had a feeling that I might be interested in meeting a healer in Cusco; for the last year I had taught a meditative type of hands-on healing called Therapeutic Touch at our medical center and he had been one of my students. Last night, just as I was dosing off to sleep, I remembered this little scrap of paper, and that Alejandro would help me find him.

The packed train ride to return to Cusco was another adventure. Every seat was taken, and full-skirted women walked the aisles selling hot tea and coffee in water rinsed cups fresh from the mouth of the last customer. "Cafe. Te.... Coffee. Tea," she sang out in a melodious high note for the Tea. More women wandered the aisles singing out *"Galletas. Dulces. Chiclets,"* carrying trays of candies, gum and cookies for sale. Passengers sat on the floor on top of their treasures rolled up in big red, green and yellow woven blankets. The trail to the toilet in this car was not going to be an easy one. I decided I didn't have to go — yet.

Rumbling down the track, the view of the dry naked mountains dipping into lush green valleys was spellbindingly magnificent. We stopped at eraser-sized villages to pick up a passenger or two here and there, and they squeezed into whatever car didn't have someone hanging off the step — veteran travelers, so no obstacle would prevent them from reaching their goal. They were entrepreneurs with pots bundled up in blankets, visiting family to an aging mother, solo children on their own; some selling chiclets, and some running away from drunk, abusive stepfathers.

My bladder suddenly decided to holler out its warning at the last set of bumps — *Get up and go now, or else!* OK, I have got to brave this after all, I thought, and stood up to make my way through the earth-fragrant coach to the toilet at the other end.

I stepped carefully trying to place my feet between arms and legs now mingled all over the floor, and nearly stepping on the face of a baby feeding at the breast of its mother. Inside finally, I closed the door and locked it. The toilet served its purpose and made my bladder happy and wiped away my imagined embarrassment of standing over my own puddle. Inside I found a treasure — a big open window with an unobstructed view of everything outside and fresh mountain air in my face. I loved it and stayed until I heard the door handle wiggle, a sure sign that someone else was threatening to leave a puddle. The trip back was uneventful, as I knew where to put my feet this time and paid more attention to the faces sitting on their precious goods.

Our bus dropped us off at the Hotel Libertador to again get settled in our rooms and reclaim our other bags from storage. Our trip was almost over, and I sighed with regret. There was so much more here I wanted to know. Never did I expect Peru to touch me the way it did. I could hardly stand the wait until my appointment with my guide Alejandro at 2:00 to meet the Andean healer Ernesto.

CHAPTER **2**

Exploring Cusco Alone

"A mind that is stretched by a new experience
can never go back to its old dimensions."
— Oliver Wendell Holmes

THE MORNING MELTED away with the sights and sounds and smells of this incredible city of Cusco. Alone, I chose to wander around the Plaza de Armas to 'just feel' the land that was causing me so much inner confusion and curiosity. Buildings, churches and walls rise over Inca stone ruins, added on top by the Spanish. Layers and layers of history are evident just looking at the structures on the plaza. The enormous cold stone cathedral has a ceiling that must be 100 feet tall. (OK, so it's less, but really up there.) I am bothered by the Cathedral's exaggerated elegance in the face of the extreme poverty of the poor. I notice the gold overlaid altars after passing a poor beggar at the door hoping for one sole (penny) from a passing stranger to buy his daily bread.

One thing that grabbed me inside the cathedral was the black Christ, made in the image of the brown natives of Cusco. The locals call it 'El Senor De los Temblores' and believe in his power to protect them from earthquakes. The first Monday of Holy Week before Easter, he is taken out and placed on a decorated platform and carried on the

15

shoulders of 40 strong men, peasants and businessmen together, and they carry the bronze colored 'El Senor' (the Lord) up and down the narrow cobblestone streets of Cusco to bless the people.

Inside the Cathedral on a sidewall is a small cove where 'El Senor' rests daily when not in procession, without any gold glittering up at him. It is here that the Indians gather tightly together standing in front of a wall of lighted candles and sing their songs of adoration to the blessed Christ in their image. The regular mass is going on to the left of this group and the loudspeaker bellows out the words of the Bishop *"el senor contigo"* — but no one in this huddle notices. Drawn in by the absolute devotion I feel and see in every pair of black eyes focused on Him and the gentle crooning that caresses my ears, my heart splits and I am weeping next to a woman in full layered skirts and long black braids. Her soft eyes look my way and continue to chant something I don't understand in Quechua. I am utterly deeply moved by their love and my emotions pour all over and down my shirt. I don't understand one word of Quechua. Yet, I feel so much here? What is it I don't remember — yet my soul does?

Meeting Ernesto

Sometime in the last hour I must have sat down, but I felt like a loaf of wonder bread on its end and slumped over, stooped shoulders, as if the entire weight of humanity were perched there. Reaching for a tissue in my jacket pocket to blow my running nose, my hand fell on a crumpled piece of paper. I smoothed it out and read Ernesto — Healer in Cusco. I must find my guide Alejandro now. It's 12:00 noon and I can't wait until 2:00 to talk to him. I can't stand it another minute.

Composed again, I stepped outside the cathedral to scan the sidewalk full of squatting vendors, hoping to see Alejandro's face just pop out at me. I weaved my way through the piles of sweaters, scarves and knit caps to the other side of the street where colorfully lined blankets were on the ground displaying ceramic sugar bowls and cups, jewelry and leather pouches. *"Compra me — compra me missus."* Buy from me miss, rang out behind me as I searched for Alejandro's brown eyes in the multicolored pairs bumping into me. But no Alejandro! Why am I looking for him here? We agreed to meet at the hotel. With no Spanish, no city bearings, and no idea where Alejandro's office was, I gave in and decided I must be patient, so I stepped into a tiny cafe and ordered 'caldo de Pollo,' a wonderful, brothy chicken soup. The warm soup calmed me down and my logical brain began to work again. In an hour we would meet and try to find the healer.

I found my way back to the hotel only turning up one wrong street, and when I entered through the main lobby door he was standing there with something like a French beret on his head and greeting me with a smile. *"Do you want to go to your room first? I will wait for you,"* he asked, obviously noting something unruffled in me. I returned his smile, showed him the piece of paper, and thanked him anyway. I didn't want to waste a minute.

Back out under the 12,000 high altitude sun, my body warmed up after the anxiety coldness that had crept into my bones in the cathedral. I almost blurted out all I had felt in the cathedral, but then a small inner voice told me, *No, focus on the paper*. I explained to Alejandro that a work friend had given me the name of Ernesto, and this healer had helped his wife many years ago when she suffered from Seroche (altitude sickness) and asked if he knew him.

"Yes, I know him, but you want to see him?" he said, looking hard at my face.

"Yes please. Can we go now?" my impatience returned.

He took me to a stone building on the street named 'Portal de Panes' on the east side of the plaza. There we climbed noisy wooden stairs to the second floor where the office sign read: 'Curandero.' I understood none of it. Alejandro told me he treated people in the community, and the look on his face told me he wasn't impressed. A baby's face peeks out at us from under the folds of a rainbow — striped blanket tied to the back of a six-year-old girl wearing a dirty white floral dress over thick green leggings, as she runs past us at the top of the stairs.

On the waiting room bench sat a mother and child, and across from her on another bench sat a man with a serious scowl on his face. Alejandro spoke to the receptionist, a pretty young girl with long shiny black hair held in a clip at the neck and sitting behind a small typewriter desk. She nodded and went quietly through another door, closing it carefully behind her.

The door opened and a short squat man wearing a vest under a black suit with penetrating, almost scary looking eyes came out. Alejandro spoke to him of my interest in his work, and as he spoke the man's face lit up and transformed into a wise grin. With a grandiose sweeping gesture meant for the stage, his entire right arm swung wide through the doorway. The small room was furnished with a leather treatment table, a table with an open notebook with names written down, and shelves lined with rows and rows of liquid filled bottles, and a single wooden chair. He spoke to Alejandro, looking at me and then to Alejandro and then again to me. Those eyes unnerved me, and I felt them prick me inside when they moved my way.

"He wants to see how you work, Rae," Alejandro told me, his eyebrows up with a hundred unasked questions.

"Please ask if I may use his treatment table, and Alejandro may I demonstrate on you?" I asked Alejandro to translate to Ernesto. Alejandro nodded hesitantly to me about using him as an example and turned to translate to the squat man with the piercing black eyes.

"Por su puesto" (Of course), he said, and judging by another grand swing of the arm, it was okay.

I asked Alejandro to lay on the table for me to demonstrate my form of healing. I told him I would do nothing to hurt him and that I would simply run my hands over his body head to foot to feel his energy and that this would enable me to notice (feeling with my hands over his body, not touching him) a health problem he might have. Laying on the table, he looked at me nervously, but trusting me.

Taking a minute to calm myself and let everything else go for now, I ran my hands over him from his head to his toes. Then I returned to his knees and told him I noted something, mostly on the right knee. His expression changed to surprise as he confided he did in fact have a bothersome right knee. I then asked permission to help make it better, and he agreed. Ernesto watched this interaction and the movement of my hands without a word. When I had finished working on Alejandro and told him he could come down from the table, he told me his knee didn't hurt him anymore, and now his eyebrows were lost under the black hair that had fallen over them.

Turning to Ernesto, Alejandro began to explain to him what I had said. A wave of Ernesto's now familiar right arm and Alejandro was silent. The short man looked directly at me and told me I was a healer and that he would like to have me come work in his clinic 'consultorio' for the year, and Alejandro translated every word. He invited me to live with his family so that my needs would be met. Alejandro continued to translate but was becoming less than comfortable with the content. I was shaken by the experience, and even more so by the offer and thanked Mr. Ernesto through Alejandro. On our way out the door, I heard a woman in the waiting room ask about Dr. Ernesto and wondered about the doctor part. Alejandro almost ran down the stairs and his stance at the bottom encouraged me to do the same. Alejandro wasn't afraid exactly, but unsettled about something, and I sensed he was protective of me. Held tight in my hand was the new piece of paper with Ernesto's name, address and telephone number on it, along with a brochure about his clinic. But I was wary of this healer who felt more dark than light.

Walking back to the Hotel Libertador, Alejandro and I spoke about the old football injury to his knee. I asked him when that was, and when he answered "last year," I was taken aback. At forty something, I was surprised to hear that he still played the rough game of soccer, known as football in Peru. The walking helped to relax me, and Alejandro seemed more like his semi-serious professional self. I asked him what he thought of Ernesto, the doctor. He spoke his words slowly, like he was picking through white rice culling the rocks and discolored grains. He preferred medical doctors, he answered without elaborating, and told me mostly the uneducated went to Ernesto. I took that to mean integrative 'healers' in Cusco were treated much like in California, believed to be based on superstition and ignorance. Being a healer myself, we changed the subject.

Stanford Trek Goodbyes

When we came in, my group was gathered by the fireplace, discussing shopping finds of the day and the dinner plans for the evening. I thanked Alejandro and paid him for his services. Linda and Mary spotted Alejandro and I entering and came closer to inquire about my interesting adventure with Alejandro. Waving goodbye to Alejandro, I step-by-step shared the interesting visit to a local healer, giving no emphasis or special interest to his offer of work. Standing close to the fireplace, I warmed up quickly as we talked and removed my jacket, noting the papers stuffed in the right pocket. I laughed at the events of this trip, dismissing any thought of his offer.

Claudia and I entered the elevator, and I pushed the button for the 2nd floor. I had just decided next time to walk if I'm in a hurry, when a bouncy stop announced our floor, and we exited and headed to room #246. I had a shower and tonight's farewell party on my mind, worried that my one dress would probably be too tight now. One thing about the Andean food — it is really good.

Our bus delivered us to 'El Muki,' the best restaurant in Cusco, which tonight was presenting an authentic music and dance show for us. I sat in the middle of the long table facing the stage and band. A sexy waiter in tight black pants (showing off his tiny ass) and a white shirt had just delivered my pisco sour. Claudia, Mike, Russell, John, Steve, Linda and I all lifted our glasses with achievement written all over our faces... and cheers everyone... well done. About that time, the band began to play a beautiful flute (quena) version of 'El Condor

Pasa' and I noticed Russell sitting across from me, but in some private place, his eyes closed, luxuriating in the music.

Claudia and my interaction on this trip is a casual coolness. We know so little about each other outside of our mutual study of Therapeutic Touch Energy Healing at the annual workshops on Orcas Island, Washington, that might describe what little flows between us. Sharing a ride from Sonoma to Orcas Island one year we talked about interesting travel and when she signed up for this trek she remembered me. It was Claudia who convinced me to come and share her tent on the trail, and it is Claudia who has become uncomfortable with how I have responded to this wonderland. We share a room and we shared the tent, we sit next to each other occasionally, and wander off rarely together, but have only superficial words to share now, since asking me when we first started on the trail if I could I *keep it down,* referring doing healing sessions for fellow trekkers with sore knees and hips, and to my intensely personal spiritual contact here. I responded that we both do healing work and I was saddened that she didn't understand there was nothing to keep down; that what I experienced personally was very powerful, designed to get my attention, and I was unable to not experience it. Sorry if it embarrassed her, but I also didn't choose it — rather, it chose me. Interestingly enough, some of the group was silently participating with me, in their own way, the spiritual elegance found here in this simplicity. I later realized that she was very private about doing healing work and sadly felt this highly educated group might judge her somehow.

When the band invited me to go dancing with them after dinner, I turned the idea over a split second — ignoring the fact that it was late, the streets were dark, I didn't speak Spanish, I didn't know how to get to the hotel and didn't know where we were. Yes, I would go with them. When our dinner was over, and the group left for the bus, I stayed quietly behind. This did not go unnoticed by half of our concerned group that something might happen to me. Our responsible US Stanford guide, Mike, was not happy with my decision, but after all it was my decision now wasn't it, said the rebel in me. I felt the love and genuine concern from my new friends I had earlier labeled a bit square and told them I would really be fine and that I wanted to go dancing and the whole five-member band would be there to protect me. They smiled with effort and left.

I returned to my room around 4:00 a.m. after dancing all night and loving it. I especially enjoyed the stretch of my mind to understand what these guys were saying to me. I owned about five words in Spanish. Sometimes body language is enough, and this night it was. I learned to dance salsa, not with words but by watching and copying until I got it. Fun, fun, fun! When I opened the door, the room was empty, and a note was scribbled on the bathroom mirror in lipstick. Claudia would not be home tonight — be back in the a.m. I had an idea where she was and was glad to see she had cut loose even under the eyes of her father and brother.

Next morning in the bathroom we said little about the smeared red still visible on the mirror.

"Classy act, Claudia," I laughed, nodding to the lipstick. "Why didn't I think of that?" I continued laughing, vowing to try it sometime.

"I didn't want you knocking on doors worried about me," she responded truthfully putting out the flames.

"You're a grown woman, and time to do something outrageous once in a while without apologizing for it," I said, and meant it. I wasn't insensitive to how insecure she was around her family, but she had to loosen up.

We never mentioned it again. In fact, we hardly spoke about anything at all. The bus to the Cusco airport was a quiet one. All eyes focused out the nearest window taking in the last view of the adobe houses with President Garcia's name splashed on the side, their red roofs and the red roads, the mountains with political words like APRA stamped on them and a coat of arms with a llama stamped underneath the words. Sadness hung inside our bus. And we all felt it.

I climbed the stairs to jet powered Faucett Airlines flight #22 and took a seat. We took off the usual half hour late, as Mike knew we would, and planned our international flight for that night. An hour later, we were landing back at Jorge Chavez in Lima. As soon as I noticed the depressing sky that hangs over Lima forbidding the sun to even peek through, I knew we had arrived in Lima. Military presence was all over like flies on forgotten food. Men like swarming ants in green fatigues carrying automatic rifles slung over their shoulders looked suspiciously at everyone. Two tanks were out in front signaling something has happened or was about to happen. One look and I knew I wanted to be somewhere else.

We arrived at the Maria Angola Hotel, modern and upscale with many mirrors in the entry and were assigned our rooms. Claudia and I were in room #422. We dumped our bags in the middle of the floor, not needing to really settle in. We would only be here for about six hours, enough time to rest, repack some things and maybe shop at the little shopping alley a few yards away from the hotel. I washed my face and changed my shirt to the blue one that I had just ironed with the hotel iron. Fresh lipstick in place and I was ready to explore the little alley of goodies. Claudia thought a minute when I told her I was going out to check things out and decided to join me.

We found only high-priced boutiques in this alley; many great quality items like the big alpaca shawls at the 'Mon Ripos' shop, in the blackest black, and another in a rich navy blue. I tried it on and danced around in front of the mirror. I could really use this, I thought, and I bought the navy blue one. We wandered and admired the fantastic pottery display in the 'Sebastian' shop drooling over this one and that one, knowing that the chances of arriving in Californian with $100.00 worth of broken pieces was too likely to risk it. But then again why not, and Claudia bought a gorgeous swirling modern black design painted on white on a tall round vase. I had never seen her so ecstatic.

"*I'll carry it on my lap,*" she told me. Good idea, I thought in agreement.

It's 5:00 p.m. already, and we both decided to relax a bit before our big dinner at the 'Rosa Nautica Restaurant' at the end of a pier. Claudia carefully placed her new treasure on the floor protected by our suitcases and plopped down on the bed. I fell onto the other one and we slept for about an hour.

Peru's coast is an uninviting gray desert sprinkled with gray rocks under a gray sky. But when I saw the long pier reaching out to sea, jutting out like a pencil with a blooming sunflower on the end, I was interested. The sea has always been home to me, and had a mysterious sleeping power over me. The 'Rosa Nautica' was built as far away as possible from the ugly slate color of Peru's coast and offering fine dining to the music of nature's heartbeat pounding underneath the dining room as the waves rolled in under us. White rolls of frothy waters are lit up by long-range spotlights facing the sea, like muscles flexing in a resting body. We shared the usual last night's dinner together talking quietly and letting the ocean's lullaby take us home.

Our midnight flight out of Lima was not to be so smooth. Our flight had over-sold their seats leaving half of our group unable to get home. After 20 minutes of serious deal-making with the airlines, Mike's warm friendly face had turned stone cold. Turning to us, he laid out the situation before us. Half would go home as planned on Varig, and the other half he was trying to get on Areolenias Argentina. The key word was 'trying.' His face softened, and his shoulders relaxed from their tightly-held position when several of the group offered to stay behind and take their chances. Claudia was one of them, and of course Mike was staying behind also, giving them a little more time together. All decided, we hugged and said our goodbyes to the six smiling volunteers behind the gate.

The eight-hour flight home was a quiet private time, and the first I'd had in the last 14 days. All thoughts of Ernesto and his offer I laughed away as ridiculous; he had dark energy that gave me deeper sense of strange discomfort. A fleeting memory of the Inca trail, my first time ever - bad knees, the Indian porters and how they watched us, the solo quena in the night moving like clouds behind my closed eyes. Dancing salsa until the wee hours with the band was great fun, especially getting back past the bolted hotel door at that hour, and I felt like a disobedient teenager.

Thoughts quickly moved to home, work, family and friends and responsibilities. I could feel the weight pile on, layer by layer, as we moved home.

The Airporter delivered me to the front door of my home, dropping me, my duffle and suitcase right in front. Something was different as I looked at the abandoned house, dark and lifeless. My key knew the way and led me inside to my comfortable familiar cave. Standing in the entry next to the bags like a statue, I didn't know the routine; my rhythm was not the same. I was not the same. Lowering myself onto the first stair to the second floor, I sat and laid my head onto folded arms over my lap and cried. Who am I? The energy of Peru is an intense flowing energy and I allowed myself to receive it. This will take time to unfold.

CHAPTER **3**

My Move to Cusco in 1986

*"You have to let go of the life you've planned,
so as to have the life that is waiting for you."*
— Joseph Campbell

HOW DOES A strenuous two-week Inca Trail Trek to Machu Picchu
in the Andes of Peru change someone? It opened me up to an unknown world, and yet somehow a familiar one that tugged on my
heart with an inner reach far deeper than I understood, yet touching a
sacred knowing asleep in me. I returned to the high Andean city three
months later, naïve about so much, and with a Leave of Absence from
my nursing job to figure it all out. Before I left, concerned friends and
family called daily worried about so many things; did I have enough
money? I assured them I did for the simple life I envisioned; how
could I be so reckless and what if I lost my job? My LOA was secure;
what about loss of funds toward retirement? I replied I would rebuild
later; what if I became ill or had an accident? and I promised I would
keep my California health insurance and I did. I heard and felt so
much fear from people who love me about all the many potential
problems, and realized I could never live my life driven by fear as
so many do. The only thing we know for sure, I believe, is life will
always deliver us change in one form or another and we will need

to adjust. The news in the '80s about the danger of Peru's volatile political unrest was true. But I didn't believe it would touch me, nor did I feel any danger, but I would miss everyone more than any of us knew then. It was an unbelievably powerful pull calling me back to Peru, even though it felt like my heart was being torn out at the same time. It was hard to leave the support of family and my community of friends, but it all felt bigger than me, I had to go. I had never taken such a huge leap. With no Spanish skills or cultural understanding of the Andean people, I felt this was the bravest leap of faith I had ever taken.

I returned to Cusco with one big duffle bag that held enough of my clothes for a year. Never a fashion statement – blue jeans, t-shirts, sweaters and a few personal things were all I would need. Oh, and two pairs of tennis shoes and a warm jacket. No credit cards, check books or jewelry was needed or could even be used without inviting a hungry person to take them. Oddly, I felt immediate freedom, as if the weight of heavy bricks had been lifted from my shoulders. I must thank a friend in Sonoma who dutifully paid my few bills. Alejandro, my Peruvian guide from the trek and I corresponded by mail before I left and he found a simple clean and furnished room belonging to a friend of his for $35 a month, so I could get settled, adjust and investigate my next step. Modest is the word that comes to mind and a good experience for me; it had a bed, a toilet and a sink. I began by taking daily morning walks in the sunshine to get acquainted with this interesting Andean city and its rhythm in a way I could not as a tourist. Slow and then Slower still, it took time to get used to the altitude and learn to be alone and with no tug on my time; what a new experience this was. Yes, light and free! I met many of the street children who were curious about me and could see that I was not racing through their city and that I would be here a while. I became a regular at a plaza coffee shop I liked and played classical music and later enjoyed sitting on a bench in the park to read in the cozy warmth of the midday sun. It seemed I read only a few words when out of nowhere appeared 5 or 6 kids who had joined me, filling up my small bench and sitting on the ground all trying at once to teach me Spanish, and enjoying how I messed it up. They also taught me naughty words, I later learned when I repeated them embarrassing myself. Really bad words I discovered, that little kids should not know.

Meeting the Street Children

Children have always been attracted to me, maybe because they can tell I like kids, and these abandoned street children became my sidekicks, and through these street kids a wide door opened up to me, and a strong loving force pulled me through.

These kids lived in a raw and brutal level of society where human beings did awfully mean things to them. Often, drunk men peed on them in the dark of night. Most street kids knew and lived only one level of society — the lowest. They set hair on fire, stole your socks without removing your shoes (although they eventually got them too), stole food and shared it with a hungry friend, and sometimes even sold their bodies for a *pollo a la Braza* (BBQ chicken). They were forced to pay the older thieves and share their take with the police. When they had no money or goods to pay, a few came to me with their bruises and oozing wounds. They eventually shared their hard-to-hear stories, their lives and their lies, and they told the truth too. They hung around to keep me company and in time grew to trust me. They protected me, and they won my heart.

During my first days in Cusco, it was some of the raggedy street children who stole my daypack with my emergency contact, camera, journal and a guidebook for Cusco. These same kids later took me by the hand to protect me by guiding me away from dangerous streets where they saw something I didn't see. They taught me Spanish and some Quechua, including all the gross words they could muster up, and I spoke them proudly to my Peruvian friends. My friends pursed their lips and lowered their eyes to cover up my numerous social errors and finally corrected me.

A tender age still, they lived a desperate life sleeping in piles to keep warm on cold cement in doorways and stealing food for survival and telling sad stories to tourists for a meal, for clothes, for shoes, etc. Yet, when I was sick, they brought me stolen food and sang Quechua songs to cheer me up. My head and values were like scrambled eggs. My heart blew open. All the rules were different here, and during moments like these the USA felt very far away. I was learning a little more every day, softly and raw, from these wise and wild kids. Mostly all were boys, but I knew some girls too. My naiveté was shattered, but I had only a taste of the world these kids were born into.

My new young friends (6- to 12-year-old boys mostly, and a few at-risk tween girls) lived a painfully difficult life for me to even witness, yet they lived it and survived by their wits, and somehow most did, but some also died of neglect. Hunger, hypothermia, bad habits, drugs, loneliness and a deep hunger for love, like all children, were all too present and they did the best they could. There were small bonded groups who, when not fighting over money, shoes or other items, sometimes helped each other. The more I got to know the kids and witness the indifference of the Peruvian Government not willing to lift a finger to help them, I was pulled through that door a little more. They suffered abuse by adults and the police who didn't protect them, and instead robbed from them and demanded a cut of any money they had and physically abused them. I spent many nights at the police station to rescue kids from the police.

These were my teachers, and I learned. I slowly stopped judging everything I saw and came to understand more the reality of the different layers of society I was experiencing.

Within six months I could communicate short thoughts in Spanish, and I understood more of the Andean people and their reality. I was just beginning to understand what I was allowed to experience by the end of 1986, my year to live in Cusco, to learn and understand what was driving me. I had given over my fear to a higher power and made a solid commitment to do something for these abandoned children living alone by their wits. How and what I would do, I didn't know yet. My heart would lead the way. There was still so much I didn't understand.

My New Aussie Friend Phil and I, Desperate to Speak English

"Rae, are you up?" he whispered, tapping softly on the door. I croaked a yes and opened the door quickly, jumping back under the warm blankets and pulling them up over my long-johns to my neck. Sitting on my one chair, he silently studied the lineup of mismatched shoes alongside my bed. My tiny rented room and saggy twin bed had a shuttered window to the side street of the plaza that provided never-ending and often disgusting late night entertainment. My green military duffle stuffed with all my worldly possessions sprawled in front of the window, its contents spilling out all over the floor.

"What's with the shoes?" (lined up next to my bed) he asked, with a silly smirk on his 30-year-old spectacled face, forgetting why he had come.

"Ammunition to throw at the mice," I answered, noticing the mice had a fiesta in my duffle last night. "They run all over in here when I sleep, and they eat my clothes." I groaned.

"Nice place you have here," smiling and raising his bushy eyebrows at the seedy surroundings.

"Where is the bathroom?" he continued.

"Down the hall to the left," I explained.

"Here, take this padlock for the door and you can plug up the holes with this paper," handing him the lock and toilet paper, ignoring the horrified look on his University of Sydney, English Professor face.

"Careful where you step, Phil," I called after him, snuggling under a bit longer to avoid the cold.

I met Phil five months after I arrived in 1986, through a fellow English language teacher, where I taught English at Cusco's 'Excel Language School.' In order to meet local people, I was teaching

English at the school for a month for 90 soles (about $30 then). Meeting another English speaker satisfied my need to speak English and stop the Spanish headaches from the overdose of immersion learning. We both agreed we needed some time off and away from constant Spanish and a friend to share our experiences in English. We became good friends and talked a lot about the large number of children living on the streets and our experience living in Cusco. Phil was on Leave from the University of Sidney, Australia, where he taught English, to travel South America for a year, but never left Cusco. His rented room with a local family included some meals and was just south of the plaza and was comfortable. I moved a few times to find a rental that I could live in.

Living in Cusco in 1986

While walking home after my last night of work as a lousy English teacher, I ran into Ivan on the street and we decided to share a pizza together. The idea of eating a real pizza sounded too good to be true. And it WAS too good to be true. But the so-called pizza was tasty and a treat nevertheless.

Between mouthfuls of a thin layer of cheese dotted with specks of ham on flat bread, Ivan cautioned me about his Cusco. He told me not to set my daypack down without holding onto it, and to watch my pockets because his people were very poor, and my white face told them I wasn't. He told me to protect my legal documents from theft. He told me about the university and the political activism against the government. He told me to be aware and watch my back. There was a lot he didn't tell me, but his seriousness made me understand. He told me there is incredible history here and where to find the best of it. He told me about the healers, the Curanderos (healers) the real ones, that they are campesinos (peasants) and are not for sale, and he told me about the others who are. He told me about popular movies from my country found outside of the main center, and he offered to take me to one. He told me about a game of Sapho, (frog) in a Chicharia (Corn beer bar) and asked me if I wanted to play. He told me only that he lived with his family nearby, that he studied tourism at the University and guided foreigners when not in class. He told me he spoke Quechua, English, and Italian and was learning Japanese when I asked, and I was astonished. He told me about the local fiestas and dancing Huaynos (local fast-step dance) and that I would like them. He told me I was different than other gringas and smiled. All this he told me in English, and the way he made English sound made me smile back. I realized I had much to learn in this unusual and rich country. The pizza finished, we walked out into the chilly night. The plaza was alive with foot traffic and street vendors selling hot rice, fried eggs and French fries out of pots balanced on lit primo stoves, and open shops. On the dark side street toward my new home human figures stood in the shadows. Without asking if I was afraid to walk alone, Ivan accompanied me to my apartment two blocks away, through an ancient and huge broken-down wood door, and down a dark alley to my door. He said goodnight with the customary kiss on the cheek used for greeting and parting and left.

Inside, I threw the bolt, turned on the light, and surveyed my home. My modest life here cost $80 month and more than most locals could afford, and that included everything. My borrowed wicker sofa and chair against the wall had green floral garden-type cushions and it was comfortable. A round table was parked between them and was just big enough to hold a small lamp and my wallet sized portable cassette and radio player. Another low wood table in front of the sofa was my coffee table. On the opposite wall was a mounted sink with cold water. Against it was a wooden table filled with my dish drainer, and two-burner kerosene pump stove. You had to pump to get just the right amount of pressure, then light it right the first time to avoid flooding and wait for a good flame. It worked well enough once I got used to it and reminded me of living on the boat.

On another nearby wall were small bags of rice, sugar, quinoa, lentils, vegetables and salt and pepper piled in a plastic bucket on my multiuse kitchen table pushed up against the wall. A can of tuna and jar of elderberry jam were the only non-plastic containers against the bucket. I had three dishes, three bowls, two mugs, a frying pan, a pot for soup and a drip coffee maker for making very concentrated coffee to mix later with hot water or hot milk, a custom I learned to love, all piled up in a corner on the other side, leaving enough room for me and a guest to eat sitting on the two wood stools nestled under the front side of the table.

On the remaining wall was a bookcase that held all my treasures — everything else: novels, books on the Incas, Spanish language texts, eight cassettes of my favorite music, rubber-banded letters from the USA, and my journals.

I had a bathroom with a sink and toilet (without a seat) and a showerhead directly over the toilet that when used gave a cold shower not only to me but also to everything else in the room. There was no hot water.

I was almost wealthy here, for I had a separate bedroom and a toilet. In my sleeping room was a single bed piled high with five alpaca blankets on short sheets and a lumpy cotton mattress, sagging from my body weight and supported only by wires stretched crisscross under it. The only light was a lamp on a small square table with a drawer next to the bed, and there was a four-drawer dresser against the wall. On another wall I hung pegs, lots of them, and hung everything on them: coat, umbrella, shirts, thick alpaca sweater made in Cusco and my hat.

At night, my bedtime ritual was to heat water in a small electric hot pot I brought from the states that required a transformer (and that I wouldn't sell for any price) for hot *manzanilla* (chamomile) herb tea and to wash my hair. Quickly, I would don thick cotton long-johns, wool socks, gloves, neck scarf, and beanie to warm my head. Only my eyes and nose were left to freeze. Cold is really cold here. My current favorite book ready on the bedside table, I would fill my white metal mug with steaming liquid, hot enough to almost burn my insides, and climb under the heavy mountain of blankets. There was no heat within these 18-inch, thick-walled adobe houses of Cusco. I would light the candle on the table and open my book. I would read this way and write in my journal until around 11:00 and fall asleep. I slept deeply, and my dreams were rich and otherworldly.

The roosters sounded like they were under my bed, waking me at 6:00 a.m. with a start at first, but in time I preferred them to the insult of my shrill alarm. Every morning my numb nose felt like a blob of ice sitting on my face, and it took a half hour bustling around trying to warm up before I could feel it. My morning ritual was a slight variation and went like this: plug in the hot pot, heat the kerosene stove placing a pot of bathing water on it to heat, and open the front door to let the morning sun warm me while I huddled on this warm spot sipping my tea. Cusco was still freezing in the morning, and the best way to warm up was to get moving, so I learned to shower faster than a GI shower using about three liters of hot water. Towel-rubbed to both warm and dry me fast, I was dressed in jeans and turtle neck polo in minutes and back to the open-door sunspot munching on delicious local flatbread and coffee, the typical breakfast. Sometimes I ate the fresh bread plain, and other times I loaded on a tasty purple loganberry jam I occasionally found in tubs in the market. Today was laundry day, so I heated another pot of water on the burner. I gave up washing with unheated tap water after the first week without a second thought to the cost of kerosene. My hands screamed in pain when immersed in the icy soapsuds to scrub my filthy jeans, and my joints developed a constant ache only soothed when dipped in hot water. I would pay the price for kerosene. The altitude sun thawed me as I slowly hung my hand-wrung clothes to dry on a line behind my rooms. From then on, my hands only hurt when I watched all the Indian women lined up on the river bank scrubbing their earth-covered family's clothes on the rocks by the side of the river, their hands cracked, swollen and bleeding, and still they scrubbed. Stark poverty did not provide for the cost of kerosene to heat the water.

I wanted to experience freely this culture and chose to live the simple life as I have described above that was actually not that difficult for me. The kids found me easily in this humble barrio and no one blocked them from visiting me, like they would in the more upscale gringo apartments in Cusco. My schoolteacher landlady, kept a girl unschooled as a domestic in her large home and repeatedly insulted me for allowing these girls to come into my tiny temporary home. As a woman alone it was not hard to meet the neglected young girls who would follow me around all day, let me wash their hair, remove their head lice nits and cook with me. I learned a lot from them as they giggled and laughed at how clumsy I was with a dull paring knife and then showed me the way to peal a potato fast. They knew their value was measured by their domestic skills of cooking, caring for siblings and washing clothes. Verbal insults would fly in their direction if discovered they couldn't cook well. As my Spanish improved I met young women who opened up to me and broke my heart just listening to the pain and hopelessness they lived in and could not escape. A woman's life is limited, oppressed and painfully hard here. I learned that men suffered their share of insults and pain too and often take out their frustration on women they have power over. With no education, no work for unskilled or inexperienced men and no chance of pride in any male accomplishments most despaired without hope and alcoholism and depression consumed them.

My day was filled with chores, and I passed the morning walking to the market for purple berry jam, two eggs, cheese and fresh bread, and learning about this culture. I talked to the women in the big San Pedro market, concentrating hard to understand every word, though at first it was the toothless warm smiles and helpful gestures from those in big white top hats over gentle brown eyes filling plump faces that got me through the day. Lugging reusable plastic woven bags of supplies, I walked the ten blocks to my home every day. I had no refrigerator. By noon, hot quinoa soup was boiling away in my makeshift kitchen and my stomach was responding to the smells that promised something good. And it was good. I discovered that I not only really loved this custom of hot soup every day, I had become a good soup maker. This too was part of my daily ritual.

The afternoon was one of rest for everyone but me. I wasn't used to resting for three hours on a sunny afternoon, so I wandered through the city and explored away from the Plaza. I met the locals and learned. I saw people celebrating a birthday, a new baby, a holiday, sitting in a circle outside in the sun eating off plates on their laps or drinking from a shared glass going around the circle, brown liter bottles of beer in front of each man. Usually these were men sitting in these circles and the women served them. The women seemed to have a very different life. I wanted to meet the adult women, but they were the hardest to get to know. They were less available and always busy with domestic work, where the men were always available, and it appeared never busy. As I walked, I met Alejandro, my guide from the trek, on the street as he hurried by on his way to meet a tour group. He stopped long enough to ask how I was and to invite me to his home for his birthday on Saturday. I accepted immediately, thrilled I would meet a local family. *"I will send someone for you at 3:00,"* he said, and hurriedly walked up the street.

The desperation of the women of Cusco living in stark poverty were everywhere and were always working, washing, cooking, bathing children, tending to children, packing their harvest on their backs in hand-woven blankets, carrying bags of food home from the market, and tending to the family and men in their charge. Their domestic chores begin when they are old enough to walk and carry a small bucket of water or a container of kerosene. They wash clothes and cook with their mothers for their brothers and father and other men in their family. They collect wood or dung on their backs for fuel.

Men gather in huddles to talk, play football and sit in circles and pass the glass of 'Cervesa Cusquena' beer or homemade Chicha (local fermented corn beer) while telling their stories to each other. At first, they laugh; then when the bottles are empty, they are crying, and their stories no longer make sense. As young boys, they learn to kick balls in a pasture and huddle with others to shoot marbles. In the Andean city of Cusco where most have come from more rural agricultural work, there is no work for the illiterate and uneducated rural immigrants in the city, no money, and eventually no food. But somehow there is always money for drink.

Outside of the city, the farmers had work; they lived with the rise and set of the sun and used fewer candles in the night than I did. Still, the men appeared to have more time to gather in small circles on simple wood chairs or just sitting on the ground with the plastic containers of *chicha* (Andean corn beer) in front of them. At least here the women stopped working occasionally and even joined their men.

Calling Home in 1986

Having too much free time allowed me to occasionally become melancholy thinking about my sons and circle of friends and the comfort of our times together. Some days I was so homesick and lonely I couldn't stand it anymore, and I would brave Intel Peru, the worst attempt of a telephone system I had ever experienced. But, then again, I was grateful there was ANY means of communicating with home.

My excitement would grow with each step down the hill from the rooms where I lived. By the time I walked the two blocks under the cold morning sun to *Avenida Sol* (Sun Ave) and the phone company, I was bursting, not sure whether to laugh or cry.

Buenos Dia. Una llamada internacional a USA, por favor (Good Morning, A call to the USA please), I said, and put my 15 soles on the counter. The clerk took the money and told me to sit down, without ever looking at me, and they would call me. Wooden chairs were lined up against the long walls with a couple of benches here and there and every seat was taken by western-dressed native men and long black hair braided on women in traditional layered skirts with glazed-over eyes. Some eyes were leaking wet, but others talked while looking nervously around the room in jerky glances. Other men and women stood or sat on the floor.

Arequipa numero cinco, the clerk called out over the microphone. An Indian woman jumped up off the floor and ran to booth #5. Then

37

came another and another while I waited, hopeful. I heard calls for Lima, Puno, Tacna, Puera, Iquitos — every town in Peru — but none for the United States. I waited some more. Waiting is something I learned to do a lot of in Cusco and something the Indians have down too well. I have seen a peasant just in from the country forced to stand for hours outside an official's door saying *Urgente* (Urgent) with watery black eyes but no other facial expression to reveal his tension. He was used to pleading, and waiting, and being pushed, and being ignored, and refused entry to cheap restaurants, and being looked over with disgust. He was used to it, and he would never be able to shake it off.

USA, the voice belted out, and I was up and ran to the desk. I didn't hear a booth number. *No hay linea* (there is no line), he said, still not looking at me and it means: there is no line, no connection today. I turned away, mouth quivering and water about to spill down my face from disappointment and from outrage — something I learned a lot about during my time there. No one cared if I spoke to my son, my friend, or if the woman squatting on the floor got through to her family, or the man standing for the last half hour ever was notified his call couldn't be made today. Everything inside was confused, and I suddenly hated this place that yesterday I loved with a passion. The crisp, clear blue-blue sky and cool fresh air that I sucked into my lungs didn't help. Not today. Nothing would help today.

Knock it off Rae! Where is your ole spunk? (talking to myself). Then, again, I REALLY wanted to hear my youngest son Lenny's voice and talk to my friend Tessa. I will try all day today if I have to until I can get through. By the end of the day that clerk would know me by my real name instead of calling me USA.

My Private Guide Alejandro's Birthday Party

Elvin knocked on the door at 3:30 p.m. to collect me for his dad's 45th birthday party. I was wearing my best and most colorful fuchsia shirt over clean black cotton pants and black flats, hoping I was not too underdressed for a party, Cusco style. For the nine blocks to his parents' home I tried to talk to Elvin, but he wasn't much of talker. He said he hoped I would like the party. He added that his wife Sonia was cooking at his father's house. Good, I thought, I will meet a woman.

Alejandro smiled broadly when he saw me and kissed me on the cheek in the customary way, oozing his pleasure that I had come to his party. He introduced me to Jaime, his brother-in-law, and two other well-dressed couples who had just arrived. A few older men in suits were engrossed in conversation on chairs placed in a circle around the living room and smiled quickly, gesturing for me to sit down, but didn't notice that I didn't, so intense was their serious political conversation. No other women were to be seen, and when I asked Alejandro if I could help his wife, he answered, *"No, no, no, no, you just be comfortable."* But I insisted, and he hauled me off to the kitchen where five party-dressed women were chopping and grinding and liquefying food. All eyes turned to me and my attire without so much as a wrinkled nose, beaming slanted eyes over big smiles of welcome to me. You would have thought it was my birthday from their expressions. I begged to help them, and in unison they told me there was nothing more to do, and asked me to please be comfortable; and judging from the site of the little kitchen, I gathered it was not polite to let a guest into a working kitchen. I returned to the other two couples now seated and talking stiffly; the older men still deep in solving Peru's serious problems. I privately agreed that somebody had better, and soon.

Noise at the door caught my attention as several more women in high heels and shiny dresses came in with more men in suits. They brought with them a bouncy joking spirit and the room was quickly transformed into voices, laughter and salsa. The women from the kitchen appeared with trays of small oversized shot glasses filled with something green and handed one to everyone in the now-full room. It was sweet and smooth, and I was thirsty. Soon another woman from the kitchen came out with another tray of stemmed glasses filled with peach-colored, tangy-sweet spiked fruit juice passing them to all. It occurred to me that these new-to-me hard alcohol cocktails might hit me hard in this altitude, but then I watched the others down the sweet stuff and decided it had little alcohol. Alone in Cusco, I chose not to drink alcohol in this altitude and was trapped here.

Alejandro told the group to dance waving his arms as if to lift them out of their chairs and then asked me if I knew how to dance 'Hauynito,' (the same local Hauynos dance step that Ivan mentioned? I wondered.) "No," I told him. "Good, I will teach you," he offered, stomping his chubby feet in a rhythmic rat-a-tat-tat motion, encouraging me to copy him. The other dancers had joined in and it appeared were all on pogo sticks and rat-a-tat-tatting next to us. I ratted, and I tatted, and then I had to stop a minute and breathe. Then I'd go again until I had spun around and around and was beginning to fear I might be sick if I didn't sit down. Alejandro returned me to my seat and the older man in the suit attached himself to me and we continued the physically grueling exercise. Alejandro danced with his heartier stout wife, and they went through the steps and passes with obvious experience and joy. Finally, back to a chair, I decided the sweet little cocktails were really 'boiler rooms' in disguise and I had better eat something.

As if reading my mind, the women appeared from the kitchen with heaping plates of food, one for each guest. I need something to eat, I thought, but this is a whole buffet on each plate. Little legs hung over the edge of both sides of mine, and those legs were attached to a disgusting head, complete with buckteeth. A fat green chili was stuffed with chopped vegetables and fried in batter, like a chili relleno, but fatter. Sliced raw onion, cucumber, and tomato snuggled next to two whole potatoes and a sliced piece of enormous kernel corn still on the cob. Glancing up carefully at the rest, I discovered all had just dug in fingers and all starting with the BBQed rodent on top. Every eye turned to me and their beloved Cuy (guinea pig). I had just the right amount of alcohol in my system to try it and gritting my teeth I bit into the black skin. It was like eating shoe leather, and in the years to come in Peru I never changed my opinion of this treasured national delicacy. The potatoes helped enormously settle my stomach and my spinning head. Just when I thought the party was winding down, the women appeared with a tray of those tiny glasses again. This time I said no and thanked the woman holding the tray. Alejandro appeared just then and insisted I have one to *brindar* (toast) his birthday. There was no escaping and I drank it down, the tasty little bomb. Then came another and another, and if there was a birthday cake or not at Alejandro's party I will never know. I was lying down on someone's bed... resting... face down. I had exceeded my limit of this fruit juice firewater, and it really hit me in this altitude. Someone took me home, and that was that. The next day I remained resting in bed with what felt like an ax in my head. I hoped not to see Alejandro again until my red face had a chance to fade a little. I learned that altitude and alcohol were not a good idea for me. I needed to always stay in control.

Lying there hung-over, I realized I had not had the chance to get to know the women. They were just not available or social outside of their comfort area like the men were. Women were kept on a short leash here and didn't venture far from the kitchen and serving the men and other domestic chores. I had been in Cusco for three months and had only been able to meet women at markets or in stores doing business, or briefly as with Alejandro's wife. I didn't even know her name. Men, however, were a very different story. I had met many men here and conversed as best I could with my poor Spanish, and clearly understood that most were married and available as if single men. I was frustrated and more than a little lonely for the genuine female company I had hoped to find at this party.

The next morning, I only wanted to stuff a sock into the empty space in my middle. Forgoing the shower ritual, I washed my face in icy water, brushed my teeth until they hurt, threw on my jeans, tennis shoes, sweater and daypack and headed to Cafe Halley for breakfast and a visit with my new friend and Cafe owner Marta.

The cafe was warm and inviting, and the 'cafe con leche' was the best in town. I ordered my favorite egg, tomato and cheese sandwich on the still fresh Cusco round bread. Marta was bouncing up and down like a yoyo tending her customers and doing the social dance with her regulars. I pulled out my journal and filled a few pages when Marta's children, Marelena and Jorge, joined me to have breakfast. Their dad ran the travel business next door and came in just then. My intense Spanish lesson was about to begin, putting the journal back in my pack.

This is the family who taught me the etiquette of Cusco, especially around Spanish language. The growing numbers of children living on the streets of Cusco who hung around with me and walked with me to the market continued to teach me words in Spanish and Quechua as we walked. I shared my new knowledge in 3- or 4-word sentences to the family and was quickly hushed, horrified and laughing at the same time as they looked all around in the café to see if anyone heard me. The street kids were having a good time at my expense it seems and taught me mostly crude words I should not repeat.

My baptism to the life and language of this incredible culture was just beginning.

CHAPTER 4

I Will Never Forget This Young Woman — 1986

"Some people come into our lives and quickly go. Some stay for awhile and leave footprints on our hearts, and we are never ever the same." — Flavia

MAYBE IT WAS the disheveled and desperate young woman, worn-out and old well beyond her years, who approached me on the street holding out to me her swaddled newborn. She was offering her tiny baby to me, speaking softly in Quechua, her mother tongue I didn't understand. But I understood her too well, sadly. She knew this much in English: *"how much?"* She needed to sell her baby. She may have had other children she could not feed and needed money for survival. Her eyes were clouded and too dark— dead eyes under a furrowed brow. She was beyond tragic in her desperate cry for help.

Her dilemma broke my heart and it changed my life then and there. I did not and could not take her baby, but I could do something to help the thousands of abandoned kids on the street.

HOW I didn't yet know, but I trusted it would become clear soon. I am a mother, a nurse and I was raised to believe I could do anything if I put my mind to it. In addition to all that experience offered me,

43

it was a passionate heart decision that I take the next step. In all these years I cannot shake the image of this poor woman. I recalled often: *'There but for the grace of God go I.'* These desperate mothers were unable to stem the flow of child abandonment. Maybe I could generate some energy to make a difference here.

By 1987, many helping hands joined to create a garage sale, collect donations and fundraise with friends in Sonoma, California, and the non-profit 'Chicuchas Wasi' (The Children's Project) was founded. CW provided an emergency shelter and love–filled home, with hot daily meals, first aid, and as a legal liaison for these mistreated and often abused kids. I lived in the shelter with the kids, set it up as a 'home environment' and guided its direction. My Australian friend Phil and I met in Cusco in 1986 and he was back teaching in Sidney. I remembered our conversations and that he was also smitten with the abandoned kids of Cusco, so I called him to see if he could get away for a few more months in Cusco to live in a house full of kids. He thought it over and called me the next day saying he would come and joined me to set up the shelter facility and help deal with the paperwork for a Peruvian non-profit Foundation. Happily we accomplished a lot together and he stayed 10 months.

The incredibly resilient children forced to live by their wits on the streets of any country is a terrible abuse of these trusting innocents we adults are here to protect. I have learned so much from them.

Imagine for a minute…

YOU were born of your mother onto a thin straw mattress on the hard-packed floor of a one-room adobe. In the corner is a small rammed-earth stove fueled by animal dung and ready so that your mother can prepare a meal out of whatever is available for your sisters. Three used candles lie on the floor next to the stove for light at night. There is an empty basket for vegetables and nothing else. Her man is gone and now it is up to her to feed your two sisters (under three) plus you. She cries as she looks upon you sadly — another daughter. She believes all females are destined to suffer — if only you were a boy you would have a better life. This mother has no skills, she is uneducated and is unable to provide for her children. She is desperate and might give YOU away.

This is not your story, but it is for some of our girls. Those of us women reading this did learn to read early and were educated. Women who can at least read have more possibilities and can learn skills to survive.

Street Children Everywhere

If I could paint youth, I would paint wide-eyed innocence and curiosity, ignorance and fantasy. A time of freedom that is, if you are very young and protected.

The street child presents a different picture of youth; like a hard-shelled walnut is encased protecting the tender complicated and undulating softness inside.

The street child sees the horrors of life and moments of ecstasy. He loses. He gains. He laughs. He is too young, and he is too old. He cries for simple reasons the privileged wouldn't understand. He has felt wet pee sprayed on his back while sleeping in darkness on cement in a cold doorway. He knows the closeness of friends and comrades, piled together for safety and warmth. He knows to slide a wallet from a jacket inside pocket, while laughing with the owner. He enjoys Chinese fried rice, knowing no particular flavor. He knows cramping stomach pains, of hunger in the night. He knows ugly night prowlers. You pay the price — you get the powder.

He knows them all — the hunted and the hunter. He feeds clients. He is fed tasteless Chinese fried rice. He finds men looking for fast women. He watches. He finds men looking for men. He watches. He finds men looking for boys. He fears. And he watches. He is used, abused. Discarded. Until next time. He knows fear — especially about next time.

He runs. He hides. He cries. Then sleeps safe and warm in a doorway, huddled with his friends. No one talks. Everyone knows. He sniffs, sniffs, and sniffs again to forget. Forget the cold, the fear. Happy, warm and drunk his brain dies, slowly. He sniffs and sniffs some more. His puffed eyes round and swollen are the whimpers of his assaulted kidneys.

He spins a sad yarn for an eager listener. He cries. He laughs. He tells of his mother's dying, beaten by a drunk in the night, her husband. The gringo listens. Tears in his eyes, pain in his gut. Eager and desperate to ease this pain, coins pass, gringo to storyteller. Coins for pinball. Coins for Chinese fried rice. Coins for "Terocol" (glue).

The street child knows truth, and he knows lies. He sees no difference; they are the same. A gift for a friend is stolen. He owns nothing. New Nike tennis shoes replace rubber tire sandals, a gift from the gringo. He parades to show them off. In the morning, they are gone. His sandals are gone. His young feet know the soft touch of the earth and the hard cold of the cement, reacquainted again.

The street child is like a cat. He watches. He learns. He strikes. He survives. He is the cat, the wise Puma.

CHAPTER 5

Invitation to a Family Lunch

"What lies behind us and what lies before us are tiny matters compared to what lies within us."
— Ralph Waldo Emerson

IVAN AND I turn away from the Plaza de Armas to walk down a shady side street where he leads me through a big wooden door the size of an ancient castle door with a smaller door inside it for people to walk through. We passed through a large courtyard where a few children were kicking a ball around in the dirt, and three small boys huddled in a corner playing tiros (marbles). Stiff-shouldered, we stepped carefully through a narrow, wet passage where outhouses weeping human waste were lined up against a wall, to another courtyard with a water spigot in the center and several children holding empty buckets waiting their turn to fill them. Deeper into the convoluted maze we wove and with a quick concerned glance at my face, Ivan pushed a makeshift corrugated-door open revealing the dark entrance to his family's living quarters.

The floor was pounded hard smooth earth, and the walls were foot-thick adobe blocks, roofed with more corrugated metal and plastic sheeting where it must have leaked during the rain. A narrow wall of shelves on the right held crowded dishes, pots, a blender, and cooking equipment — refrigerator, broken electric stove with plywood on top to make a work area, and a wooden table was tightly fitted on the left. The indispensable two-burner kerosene stove sat on the floor under the table — a curtain hung like a shower curtain blocked the view further inside.

Pulling it aside, Ivan moved inside, saying nothing to me, and I followed. In the corner on a squat stool not six inches off the floor sat an old Indian woman bent with osteoporosis eyeing me as if I were from Mars. She spoke to Ivan in the dialect of Cusco and he answered laughing, not translating for me. A long table filled this room on three sides leaving no room to move around it other than to sit on the benches. On one side of the room was a 9″ color TV under an attic type staircase leading to two beds crammed into the small overhead loft. On the other side of the table was another curtain, and behind it a windowless room with two bunk beds and a single bed jammed together against three walls. An orange chamber pot on the floor was covered with a towel. Here lived his grandmother, mother, eight siblings and father when home. The eldest sister, Lena, is a nurse and required to live at her post in a remote village, so rarely home. There is no running water and no bathroom inside. One look around, and I understood why Ivan hesitated to bring an educated Gringa from the US to his world. And I tried to hide any expression of shock at their extreme poverty.

The grandmother's eyes were never off me as the slow simple life moved inside these walls. Ivan's sister, Maria, nervously offered a forced smile and a cup of steaming mate de Manzanilla (Chamomile tea) in a china cup and saucer. I gratefully accepted the hot liquid flowing into my body to calm my first taste of poverty. The youngest eight-year-old boy was watching cartoons in Spanish while his grandmother hid behind the curtain to block the view of the TV that she didn't understand, and afraid the people or cartoons would come out of the TV and hurt her.

It was time for lunch and one by one the brothers filed in and took their places at the table. It was then I noticed Maria, the only female present, bustling around the thimble-sized kitchen of boiling pots on the kerosene burners. Her four brothers sat around the table with the grandmother still on her low stool, the regular chairs too uncomfortable for her bent-over body. The youngest sister, 14-year-old Ana, joined the rest at the table — a solemn daily ritual for this Andean family. Heads were not held high and the girls looked no one in the eye. Sparse conversation, sprinkled with an occasional smile or giggle, interrupted the slurping of scalding soup. Eyeing the bowl in front of me, I was stuck on the beady black eyes looking back from the liquid. The chicken broth had pieces of carrot, celery and the entire head and neck of a dead chicken. The other bowls were the same but had a foot of a chicken instead. I was the honored guest and the yummy treat was wasted on me. The sucking slurping sounds next to me were from Berto getting every bit of flavor from each toe of the foot. My chicken head just stared up at me, as if daring me to go ahead and take a bite. Grossed out, I couldn't do it. So instead I raved with umms and oohs, the only language available to me, spooning the flavorful liquid down until the naked head rested abandoned in my bowl. Without a word, Ivan stabbed it with his fork and the sucking, slurping sounds continued.

Maria served everyone as they came in, barely sitting long enough to eat her own soup. I tried to offer my help and appeared to offend her. I learned my first month in Cusco that guests never serve, and resisted the urge to help his sister. Up again, Maria was serving heaping plates of rice and vegetables while Ana cleared off the empty soup bowls. By the time she could sit to eat her own, a brother handed her a plate for seconds and she was up again. My feminist self was taking it all in and not liking the implications.

Next came coffee and small talk between family members who clearly knew little about the other's private life. I practiced my Spanish, and everyone laughed. I tried again, and they laughed harder. My social skills were nonexistent here, but I plowed along, and Ivan interpreted and explained for me.

In one hour, the family had returned from private worlds outside

49

their home for lunch, had eaten, exchanged a few words, and had gone out again to that same world, leaving an empty table and a pile of dirty dishes, pots, and pans to ready for the next meal. Only Ivan, Maria, Ana and I remained. His sisters did the cleanup it was understood, but today Ivan lifted the plastic tub piled high with the dirty mess and led the way outside into the warm sun and the water spigot. Maria followed with two buckets and an almost empty bag of powdered soap. Filled with cold water, one for wash and one to rinse, we washed up the whole lot together and relaxed into real smiles and laughter under the midday sun. Ivan was the only male in his family to lend a domestic hand to his overworked sister, and I was proud to know him. I later discovered he often cooked for Maria in the early morning, and my admiration grew.

A Gringa in this back alley was unheard of, never invited, and my visit to Ivan's home turned every head as we made our way out onto the street. Leaving, his face showed relief and contentment so that he almost skipped down the street to my house. I was trusted and have just passed a test of acceptable social behavior in this poor community. I am sure there will be other moments where I will be observed carefully to see if I am respectful of the people who welcome me and I try to be always.

CHAPTER 6

Chicuchas Wasi Shelter Opens

"Do not wait for leaders; do it alone, person to person."
— Mother Teresa

Ronald — First CW Child — 1987

CONTENT AFTER MY favorite egg, tomato and cheese sandwich and great perked coffee, I stepped outside into the warm sun from my friend Marta's café on Platero Street. Turning to head for the plaza, I see Ronald, a boy about 13 years old who lives alone on the streets, heading for me. Street kids tend to sleep late since they work most of the night. His hand was pressed over his upper right arm with a wince of pain. Sometime during the wee hours of sleep, he was awakened by other boys stealing his few possessions, and this time a knife appeared in the hand of one of the boys. Trying to protect his belongings against the boy with the knife, his arm was sliced. After a quick look hours later at this dried up, bloody and dirty mess, we were off to the ER. The wound looked deep and needed to be cleaned and sutured. He couldn't sleep on the streets like this and would have to come with me.

Taking a breath from my rescue mission, I realized this boy could not go to a pension with Phil and me while we hunted a permanent

CW location, no matter what happened. Phil would be returning to Cusco from Lima today and would agree. My friend Marta was watching and saw the situation unfold. She thought for a minute and told me I could not take him to a pension with me and that it was safer for me to bring him to her little apartment with Phil until CW had its own place. She told me I was coming to her house where she lived with her daughter and son since separating from her husband. She lived in a small three-bedroom apartment — one room for her, one for her daughter, and one for her son. I teamed up with her daughter, and Phil would team up with her son, and Ronald had a cot in the kitchen. This was how CW began, with the generosity of a caring, local businesswoman. This was powerful and generous support from a local family for the CW Shelter, to provide for these children in need, and rare during my 10 years in the Shelter.

Several days later, another local friend said his father heard of a condo type apartment that would give us a place to live as we began CW. Two weeks later the papers were signed, stamped and recorded and I paid the money sent from my personal account to close the deal. CW Shelter had a place to begin.

Ronald was the first member of the CW shelter and could now sleep in a safe environment. No one would hit, knife, kick or pee on him in the night. It was warm, and the bed was soft. He could sleep soundly.

Beds, Pots and Pans for the CW House

Immediately we were in need of basic furniture and were directed to the local outdoor impromptu market where we began to buy bunkbeds, blankets, a bed for me and one for Phil, pots, dishes and a two-burner kerosene stove. Neither Phil nor I knew how to use the scary kerosene stove. Ronald did, and he showed us how. This common cooking tool became our cook-top outside on the patio against the back door. Flames flew up three-quarters of the way to the top of the door and quickly turned it burned black, but it cooked well once the flame calmed down — Phil and I calmed down too. The project was off and running with the basics almost in place. We had a cold shower that no one cared to use, but necessity dictated, so a common funky electric showerhead took the cold chill off the water, but you could not touch it or the pipes until you got out and dry, or you would feel the electric shock. Scary stuff. The boys and their grime were too much, so Phil had the pleasure of getting them, one by one, into the shower and using soap. He was good at this and you would have thought some sort of torture was going on with all the yelping coming from the bathroom. More children came to our Shelter little by little as the word spread.

Life in Cusco was simple, with little stress in 1987 — not simple like you would mean if you applied that to California lifestyle, but simple CW Shelter Andean style. Barebones living; sleeping two kids to a bed and all sharing a poorly-functioning bathroom with water available three hours a day and held in buckets the rest of the day to flush the toilet. We boiled frigid snow-melted water for coffee and tea and just heated water to warm the ice-water for washing clothes, and when there was water to shower, we used an electric shower device you didn't dare touch while in the shower. We cooked on a two-burner kerosene primos (a two-burner homemade cooking apparatus that most people use in Cusco), and we kept on the side patio outside the house. The flames shot up to the tile overhang when it was warming up convincing me we were all insane pyromaniacs trying to blow ourselves up. This fire ritual went on every meal since we had no other way to cook in Cusco those first years.

Death Andean Style — 1987

Barely awake, I hear the phone. *"Buenos Dias, Rae."*
"Hello, Maria," I respond.
"I think La Abuela (grandmother) has died. Can you come," she

asks. A nearby family dear to me needs verification that the grand-mother is dead.

"Yes, I'll be right over," I tell her. I jumped in my jeans and t-shirt and was out the door in 10 minutes.

She was still warm, but her spirit had gone — but not far; it lingered nearby. The three-room adobe house was empty, with only the grandmother, granddaughter and me. Everyone knew and left for Maria to prepare the body. We bathed her together; her presence still hanging in this tiny dark adobe room lit by candle light which seemed to caress me back as I gently stroked her body with a towel and warm water. I realize now that I had known long ago this old Indian woman afraid of the TV.

Spread out over the only table used for eating, cooking and study was La Abuela now surrounded by candles. Paper burned as a ritual at the door entry to this home for protection.

The grandsons accompanied La Abuela while we went to the Franciscan Convent to buy a nun's habit in which to bury her. Holding the bundle close to her, Maria led me to where the coffins were made, calls to the priest and plans the funeral.

In the center was the coffin surrounded by three-foot-tall candle-holders supporting even bigger candles. The walls were lined with chairs filled with family and close friends sitting quietly together in this cold, unfriendly room waiting for the priest — who was late. Finally, he arrives announcing he is in a hurry to go somewhere else so must hurry. He said the poor man's mass without communion and ran out the door. This poor family expected no more.

Roma, Friend and Social Worker

More Kids Enter CW Shelter — 1987

While struggling to get our double-locked door open, I heard the phone ring. Running up the stairs two at a time, I answered out of breath.

"Hello Rae, this is Roma and I need your help." Roma was a social worker and the only SW I ever met over the 10 years working with children in need in Cusco.

"What can I do for you, Roma?" I asked.

"I have two young girls in an unsafe living environment with a non-relative and need a place for them for two weeks."

Our house was full of boys and even though this presented the obvious problems for us, of course we would take them. A few hours later two young sisters, Rosa (seven years old) and Santu (about 12 years old), were standing in our entryway with a look of concern on their faces. I welcomed them to our CW family and showed them up the stairs to the 3rd floor dormitory for female adults and children. Phil and the boys had the second floor. The girls brought little with them and were quickly shown their space and beds. When I return to California I often can gather useful kitchen tools and other items needed in the Shelter. I also collect clean and good quality children's clothes on my trips to California from friends with growing kids for our Cusco Shelter supply store-room and therefore would select clothes for them later. School reg-istration, black shoes and the gray uniforms required for Peruvian public school would come first.

The girls quickly settled in and between Phil and I we watched how the integration of girls with a bunch of unruly tween/teen boys would unfold. The boys were watching the adults and the adults had an eye on the boys. The message was unspoken but clear: respect and cooperation from all would ensure a smooth and happy *hogar* (home). With the generous skill, knowledge and labor from Ivan's family, we soon modified the third floor to accommodate more fe-male volunteers and Naida, another girl about eight years old who joined CW.

I met 13-year-old Ronald a year earlier as one of the street kids who followed me around and befriended me, before we obtained the CW house shelter. Ronald was now about 14, was the first boy who moved into the shelter, and he soon found his younger brother

Fernando who immediately joined us. The word spread, and more boys quickly moved in. We had legal permission to provide shelter, but not to demand they stay. So, some came and saw the list of responsibilities and left with whatever they could stuff into their pockets. We got much tougher about telling the truth and not stealing from us after that. The first local volunteers were not always interested in the kids and were also masters at stealing themselves — canned milk, tuna, shoes and even the iron. We had to learn to weed out those whose personal need was so great that the temptation was too big to resist taking from CW.

The daily routine was still being established since there was a lot to manage in a big CW family like ours, and everyone had to participate in the chores equally, regardless of gender. One objective of the shelter was to teach basic living skills needed for a decent life. Individual responsibilities were divided and written on a big calendar. The cooking team rotation involved two kids and either Phil or I, and the kids would chop soup ingredients and put them into the pot to boil the lunch soup while the water heated to prepare the oatmeal breakfast every a.m. before school. This worked well and soon the kids were expert soup makers and created a competition — what team had the best cooks? Phil's team was at a disadvantage as his menus were limited to canned tuna with something. We had to work on that, and this soon improved. Raising three sons proved a big help to me and to the kids on my team too. Other responsibilities like rotating days for showers due to limited hours for water, oral care, daily school and homework, and Saturday's personal laundry day on the patio in big red wash buckets were planned out.

Interesting, that over the years two of our boys became the best cooks, better than the girls. So, a little competition was good in the kitchen and everyone responded when we needed to do better. Plus, it was fun.

Unsung Heroes of Early Chicuchas Wasi

When Chicuchas Wasi was created, a founding team of outstanding energized board members was formed; I gathered friends to meet and hear my story and that I wanted to do something to help these kids survive and invited any who wanted to join in this effort with me. In one way or another many wanted to help or had friends they told about this new project that could help. They all stepped up to identify our immediate practical needs of accounting, graphic design, giant garage sales, Christmas craft sales, and more. Together we sat on the floor of my friend's living room and brainstormed ideas to raise start-up funds and then ongoing funds and as we learned we would need never-to-end our fundraising efforts down the road. Most importantly, they personally took on some of CW's important and most urgent needs using their professional expertise, creating the Chicuchas Wasi founding board of directors. I will be forever grateful to all of you. I list you here for as many as I am able to get their permission to add their names in the book. Please see acknowledgements for more.

The Early team members: Karen Amoruso – CPA extraordinaire, John Lopez – passionate organizer, Mary Salfi – T-shirt sales, Iris Rasmusen – constant use of her home, Terry McDonald – Graphic Designer, Steve Burdick – Businessman, Pat Brown – loyal energetic friend, Brook – energetic team player.

John Lopez, a colleague at the Santa Rosa medical center where I had worked as a nurse, organized a huge garage sale in the enormous parking lot of the medical center. Hearing of the project start-up funds this sale was to provide, supporters cleaned out their garages and hauled their no longer needed goods to spread out all over this parking lot for other people to purchase in need of these items. Bilingual radio advertised this one-day sale, the paper put in an ad, we all called friends and family, and even sold hot dogs and soda that another co-worker arranged who knew how to do that. In the end, the unsold leftover goods were again published over the air, for free this time, and within an hour the parking lot was empty again. John delivered to me $2000 seed money to take to Cusco, Peru and begin the CW Shelter. This was 1987.

Another founding board member, Terry (and her husband Ken) were members of Rotary. The Pleasanton North Rotary designated CW as their international project, thanks to Ken (past President of this club) and Terry McDonald (CW BOD member) who worked hard to convince their members to donate funds already raised to fund the needed furnishings and materials for our new education center. *Moving forward* — A dream that was born in 1995 was realized in 2000 thanks to Rotary Club-Pleasanton of California who funded this dream. The CW computer lab of six computers and peripheral equipment became available to our students who would benefit from this technology, either as an introduction or even much later for more advanced use. Terry McDonald was also our Graphic Designer extraordinaire and created all of our beautiful flyers, big banners and cards with artistic skill over the years and still jumps in when needed since her retirement a few years ago.

Many other friends over the years brought huge boxes of kitchenware, clothes, sheets and other basics, money, peanut butter, personal items and so much more to our door in Cusco and lit up my day. There are too many to name here, but I am grateful to you all for the many generous gifts you sent or brought down, and for re-energizing me with your visit and thoughtfulness in all that you sent. The CW positions have always been volunteer positions for all of the board members and the many other generous supporters who jumped in now and again over the 31 years. I too have been a volunteer for 31 years, grateful I am able to do so.

CHAPTER 7

The Shelter Life in 1987

"Wherever you go, go there with all your heart."
— Confucius

TAKING A BIG breath: *This ought to keep me in shape.* I thought, facing the 65 deep stairs on the car-wide footpath to my Andean adobe home. I quickly learned not to be going up or down during the opening or closing of the school 'Colegio' unless I wanted to be trampled by a herd of 3rd and 4th graders.

Step-by-step, I climb, aware of the effect 13,000 ft. has on my body. Why is it some days I can sail up these stairs and scarcely be out of breath, and others I fanaticize having one of those sit-down escalators that carried old ladies up flights of stairs in the old movies. Out of breath, the pain in my chest slows down my steps just breathing to 10 steps at a time — breathe-rest-breathe another 10, then rest again.

Two doors past the school is the faded pale blue wooden security door slapped over the entrance to the adobe condo-type units. There are six apartments inside, all secured by each other, and this main entry door locked at night. I chose this apartment for the Shelter because it is only two blocks away from late night plaza activity with kid crisis and is secure.

Sadly, Cusco has a second main underground education system

— that of thievery. Locals don't leave vehicles on the street five minutes at night, knowing the expert night workers would have it disassembled and removed without even a grease spot proving there was ever a car there. I am a gringa in the land of brown-skinned look-alikes, so not unnoticed and a prime target. It's common knowledge all gringos are filthy rich and hardly notice being ripped off. The project kids are graduates of this underground school where older boys teach the younger ones how it goes. Our kids spend many nervous hours protecting me from known sharks looking for easy takings.

At our door, the keys go into the stiff double lock, one on top of the other, and I have to turn them both at the same time, careful not to break them in the lock. Click-click, I'm in. Clicking the light on in the entry hall, I see it is full of food supplies. Donations of 50# sacks of USAID flour, lentils, wheat and powdered milk is given to NGOs and we took advantage.

Not ready yet to climb up another flight of stairs to my room, I drop my pack on the stairs and head for the kitchen. The entire first floor is living room filled with a simple wooden couch with brown covered foam cushions, and matching chairs, a wooden coffee table and bookcase filled with puzzles and games and a couple of books. Pass through to the dining room and around two long tables with benches on the ends and chairs lined up on the sides. This room sees more action than a 49er football game. Vegetables are chopped here early mornings during breakfast prep of oatmeal and coffee before school. Our main meal at lunch is a morning-long process for whomever has the job today. Afternoons see busy projects; math and grammar spread papers like a tablecloth. Bread making, laughter, stories, tears and tantrums follow the evening meal. If these walls could talk…

Our little kitchen is like any kitchen in the world. Well, *almost* any kitchen, if you don't count the two-burner kerosene stove on the patio floor next to the back door. Only the kids could light this thing, and it produced flames that flew up three-quarters of the door, now entirely black from the soot. Phil and I were wrecks waiting for some terrible burns and finally found the funds to buy an electric stove with an oven. Our pyromaniac days were over. Regardless of the stove, this warm cozy spot invited warm conversation while stirring a steamy pot of soup on the much hotter kerosene burners.

Everything we did to meet our basic needs, we did together and though tedious we made it fun. The kids had daily chores — cooking with an adult, washing clothes and dishes, and baking bread were some of them. Music blared, kids checked the checkerboard calendar on the wall spelling out who had what responsibility when, and like a circus of tricks and maneuvers, we entertained one another with little theater acts in the kitchen — singing, dance steps and splashing precious water all over the one washing. Chopping, blending, and peeling were an art form the kids mastered, and their creative spirits added personal touches and carved faces in vegetables before they went into the pot for fun. Imagine the great energy of joy that went into the food we ate. The house ran like a smooth motor, efficient and orderly, in spite of the 15 kids and four adults who lived there. This is how we lived day in and day out, making fun out of whatever presented itself, and it was amazing the way these kids, rescued from sleeping in doorways on cement streets, brought happiness into the simple home we had created.

Every occasion was a party. We celebrated each child's birthday with a cake — usually I made the cake with many onlookers who wanted to learn this trick and did. There were no toys or things. Instead, we created innovative, creative ways to entertain ourselves. I doubt that we adults could top what the kids came up with.

Mother's Day was a big day and something special was always being prepared to eat, like 'Aji de Gallina,' one of my favorite Andean dishes. Then came the honoring of the designated 'Mother' by this group of motherless kids. The kids put a chair in the center of the room and asked me to sit there. One by one, the children would step forward to our makeshift stage and recite memorized poems, placing one hand over their heart and the other outstretched in grand style. The next child would step forward and sing a song acapella, and then another with another poem for me. A very touching and emotional event for me.

Coffee cup in hand and grabbing my pack, I head up the stairs to my room on the second floor now. I drew the room next to the boy's dorm with wall-to-wall bunk beds and clutter and the only bathroom — and responsible for order on this floor. The third floor is a large dorm where the one to two volunteer women and the three girls live. Part of the third floor is a storage area for extra clothes and supplies. There are two skylights on this floor adding natural light and warmth here making it the best room in the house of no artificial heat.

I have just enough time for a brief rest before everyone is home.

Weekend Chores and Baking Bread 1988

A surprise donation gave us the extra funds allowing us to purchase an electric stove with an oven. The paranoia that Phil and I had experienced was slightly appeased regarding the kerosene pump burner on the concrete patio ground and the constant reminder of danger with the completely burned door on the outside. The kids knew how to operate it, but the flames still went almost to the top of the door. Miraculously, no burns or clothing fires ever happened.

This was when I discovered the USAID program in Peru to help NGOs like ours, and I got in line with the mostly nuns working like me waiting to receive donated flour, lentils, powered milk and rice and bulgur wheat in big sacks. This was perfect timing. The house entry was often packed with these sacks of staples. The flour especially served us well and we made bread almost every day on our long wood table covered with an oilcloth to feed our always-hungry teens. The kids jumped in and took turns with Phil and I initially until Phil moved, making a floury mess of the downstairs. Add the just purchased 25# sugar — all stacked up on top of each other until we figure out where to put them.

So, began the adventure of bread making with the kids living in the CW shelter. Big smiles and laughter bursting from white-powered faces, flour covering hardwood floors with bare footprints and lots of pounding and banging until the bread dough was 'tamed.' Our workspace was directly on top of an oilcloth covering our eight-foot-long table. Five or six of us daily would pile a bunch of flour onto the middle of the table, make a well in the center, pour in the oil and Royal and mixed it all with our hands — all washed, hopefully. We took turns with much theatrics around pushing, kneading and pounding this poor dough until it could be made into a shape, or two or three. The kids' creativity flourished as figures of animals, braids and shoes and baby Jesus began to take shape and ready for the oven. The oven temperature was a guess, so HOT was our collective decision. Once, their Pan WaWa (baby Jesus) during Easter was so big that we had to cut it in half to fit in the oven, but no one cared. We just pieced it back together after baking. The attitude was that it all tasted the same anyway and having fun was the point. Eating it, of course, too.

While baking was going on, the entire downstairs smelled wonderful and the fresh bread aromas wafted upstairs to the bedrooms. Pretty soon, we became really good at our technique and would add raisons or make cinnamon rolls at times. We created and supplied all the bread for the 14-15 people living in the house. All of the kids loved the bread-making fun and soon we made two piles of dough, so they could all create. Of course, we ate it all easily in those early years. It became a sort of practical therapy and no end to the entertainment for up to 15 tweens.

When the event ended, the table, floor and kitchen were barely recognizable with all the white flour everywhere complete with footprints leading upstairs, to the bathroom, the hall and front door. Phil and I tried to impress upon all that the cleanup is part of the fun — they didn't buy that. But they did learn to clean up the mess they made.

Experiencing life in Cusco 1986

Founding Board of Directors for CW Calif. 1987

Ronald, first child to enter the CW Shelter 1987

Rosa and Santusa join the CW shelter family 1987

Rosa settled into CW family life

Phil and our wild boys of CW

Clothes washing day was mostly playing around

The Girls actually washed their clothes.

Clothesline laundry dried fast and filled the Cusco patio

Rosa's turn on cooking team-Urubamba

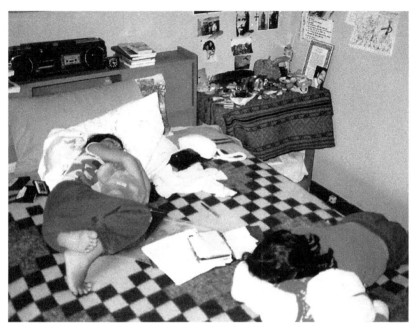

Rosa & Zenaida asleep on my bed while I typed grant proposals

American Chamber of Commerce, Peru donation to CW

Rae, Rosa & Santusa

Kids, big pots and panetone bread for Xmas outreach

Xmas outreach, Efrain serving hot chocolate to a little one

Rosa was the Princess of her primary school 6th grade

Urubamba house converted to a B&B to support CW 1991-97

UrpiWasi B&B dining room-kids lean restaurant skills

Pool fun and swimming lessons for all

Like a big bathtub-pool cleaning was even more fun for all

Maestro Juan, Efrain and Hipolito in Urubamba

More of the core kids: Santusa, Rosa, Efrain, Hipolito and Zenaida

Christmas Cookies were a big hit to create and then eat

Rosa and Santu really got into the California cookie recipes

Hipolito the artist at decorating Xmas cookies

Fun outing at the river in Urubamba

CW expert bread makers for artistic creations and small buns

Core kids in Urubamba (we lived in the B&B house 1991-98

Phil on duty in Cusco Patio 1987 with the playful CW girls

CW University kids & Ruth, Rae and Gloria to return to Cusco

Boys and Hygiene

Pre-teen boys, used to sleeping in doorways and under market tables on cold concrete, couldn't care less if their clothes were filthy or their bodies smelled. The level of life they have had thrust upon them has only given the example of what they have now. We never know how long we will have the kids we accept into the shelter. By law we cannot obligate them to stay and given that they are accustomed to their freedom to do what they want and when they please, some may or may not choose to stay. We have rules like: must attend school, wash clothes and bedding, hygiene and brush teeth daily. No stealing or lying, and finally learn to cook decent food in teams. Some of the kids are so independent they just will not stay with any rules, preferring the street and the bad habits that have kept them alive up to now.

Saturday Washing Day

To get the attention of the kids for the most unloved chores of personal hygiene and washing clothes, we had to make it fun. We taught the basic living skills needed in life to build good health, dignity and personal confidence to succeed for a quality life. Washing was believed women's work and beneath a male. But we changed that.

On Saturday mornings there is a lot of action until 11:00 a.m. when the water shuts off. The patio outside is a maze of big red plastic washtubs, low stools and scrub brushes scattered around outside on the cement patio. The tubs are filling halfway with very cold tap water, heated warm water and Ariel powdered laundry soap (lightly) so strong that holes from scrubbing can appear after one or two washings. Music blares from the radio in the window and soon fills the warm sunny patio with singing, stories and laugher. Without music, there would be no action at all. 'Ariel' laundry soap is strong for a reason in the Andes (grime is serious here) and especially needed here to tackle the boys' clothes that will enter next. The boys look to our three girls as if they're ready to jump for joy to wash the boys' clothes, as is the custom in homes. No, not in this house!

The boys' smiles vanish immediately while the girls look down to their own washing with smiles slipping across their faces as they scrub, scrub, scrub. The boys must wash their own clothes, just as everyone (Phil and I too) must wash our own.

So, the washing begins. The boys throw a few items in the tub and with a foot swirl them around and around while I head upstairs to see where the rest of their clothes are hiding. Splashing and jumping in and out of the tub for fun follows the music. There is not much wrist action in regard to the dirty clothes, only being stepped on and danced on by the boys. Many lines are strung up the full length of our small patio about 15 feet long by 8 feet wide — as many as will fit. The hot Cusco sun will dry the first batch of wet clothes in an hour, so the next batch can be hung up to dry. The splashing of feet and hands has little contact with clothes soaking in the water other than the occasional stomping on them. Not much washing from the soaked boys, but they soon realize they cannot escape this chore and give up. The girls get into the play and soon they are all soaked and have had a partial shower out in the hot sun.

Showers are the next dreaded chore that all must have at least once a week. To their delight, we often do not have water when it is there turn to shower. Central Cusco has only about two hours of water in the early a.m. and about an hour to two hours around dinner and early evening. Large plastic garbage cans sit in our useless tub to store water and use with a smaller bucket to flush toilets and wash your face. Dental care is new to most of the poor, as are baths of any kind due to the water rationing. Outfitted with toothbrush and toothpaste, we are making headway with the boys. The girls are pleased to have clean clothes, bodies, and teeth so it is a non-issue.

CHAPTER 8

Early CW Fundraising — 1987

"It always seems impossible, until it's done."
— Nelson Mandela

MY ROOM WAS one-half office and one-half bed and closet. I lived there alone, if you don't count two or three kids lying across my bed much of the time keeping me company or sleeping. It was here I typed grant proposals to mail out (paper and stamps) and other CW project work, wrote in my journal, and stared out the window at the huge white Christ alone on the Cusco hill — a gift from the Arabic Palestinians at the end of WWII living in Peru.

The first years were financially a struggle and threatened to sink my mood most days. The responsibility for all of the abandoned kids who came through our shelter doors and the reality that there was little to no possibility that I could raise funds in Cusco was depressing. Many grant proposals were written, stamped and mailed, but no one ever responded and that was hard to take, draining my energy.

Typing on the IBM Electric typewriter gifted from my California Medical center, the same proposal for the 100th time judging by the balls of wadded-up paper on the floor, my grant proposals were always rejected in a rare reply, with *"Peru is not in our area of focus this year,"* leaving me frequently desperate for funding to feed this gang.

On one particular day, my rubber band was pulled so tight it was about to snap, as I lay with my head on the typewriter, tears spilling on the keys and down my face. Paper balls covered the bed and floor. *I've run out of steam; the well is dry*, I lamented to myself on my uncomfortable headrest.

Shouts came up the stairs to me from the dining room table: *A la mesa, a la mesa* for lunch, but I was unable to move. The unforgiving typewriter only advertised my weak typing skill with too many errors to correct with whiteout and ended up ruining the documents and my day leaving a paper mess. I had come to the end of my rope and laid my head on the big ugly typewriter and cried.

There was a light knock on my bedroom door where I worked, and it opened quietly.

Rosa, then seven, looked around and gently walked over to me and laid her head on my lap and placed her arms around me. She stayed that way silently for a few minutes, lifted her head and left as quietly as she entered. That gentle act of love shook me out of my self-pity and I got up, cleaned up the paper balls covering the floor and went to wash my face. I could do better! I would do better!

I began to brainstorm again about what other approach I could try. Flying to California was a must to generate some helpful donations and recharge my batteries. My medical center always donated many supplies useful to the people of Cusco and our kids. I even received X-ray film needed to do a proper full- sized chest X-ray to diagnose Tuberculosis — endemic in Cusco.

Our Shelter budget was only $15K to $20K a year in 1987 & 1988 — we knew how to be frugal. I also traveled like a pack mule, thanks to a friend well placed with Varig Airlines in San Francisco, who allowed me all the extra weight I needed at no cost. Unlike most travelers, I went to the airport in a truck filled with big moving boxes in the bed (totaling 1,000 lbs. once) — whatever could travel down the luggage conveyor like a suitcase in Lima. I hauled a lot of the basics from California (IBM typewriter, utensils, pots and pans and kitchen stuff, books, clothes for the kids, shoes, games, office materials), and bought our first little $4K Apple computer in 1999 and later received an old Kenmore gas stove from Vancouver. I was young, energetic and strong then.

A Garage for Our Yellow Truck — 1988

I'm banging the rock as loud as I can strike on the oversized wooden doors at the garage. It's 7:00 a.m. and still they are not open. I hear footsteps shuffling to the door, fumbling for the key and chain lock finally and the big wings open wide to all the shiny metal stored inside. Like sardines in a can, they are packed in. Lucky for me mine is only two cars deep.

"This is doable — just be patient for a few minutes while I move them around, Rae." But the owner is in no particular hurry — a contrast to my watch-ordered life. He is looking for keys to the red VW bug blocking me in. Two more owners arrive to retrieve their vehicles. The owner juggles the VW to the cars on the left, now glued tight to them and signals for me to come and get mine. A narrow trail leads to the street — too narrow to pass — but this is the way we do it here. I will try. An old Dodge truck vintage 1950 is rocked back and forth, back and forth painstakingly and widens the trail another few inches.

Inside, I beg our tired Toyota truck to start up today, placing the key in the ignition and praying, *please roll over.* Click, click, click. The battery cables are not making contact, a familiar and well-rehearsed scene. I expertly slide my hand under the nose of the hood, lift the latch and open her up like a giant can lid. There is, just as I suspected, white acid corrosion around the contact bolts on the battery. Returning to the driver's side, I open the door, reach with my hand under the seat, feeling, feeling, feeling... There it is — my wrench! I return to the battery and expertly give it a few whacks. In the driver's seat I turn the key and the motor turns over and over and over and catches. Sputter sputter-sputter-varoom! The hood replaced in its locked lid down position, I begin the maneuver to leave this nighttime car jail.

Inch to the right, two forward, now to the left and I slide out of the big wing doors onto the open street. Filling my lungs down to my toes and exhaling the earlier tension, I relax into the motor's deceiving hum and turn onto the cobblestone street. The sun shines on the street warming the crisp Cusco morning air. The Andean Mountain *Apus* (Gods) surround the city as a constant reminder of their protection and strength.

I'm stuck at a red light and my watch says 35 minutes went by in the garage while we played soft bumper cars. The yellow garage sticker is placed on the dash, and I am running: lawyer, bank, Marta, SUNAT (Peru IRS), and meet Ruth at 1:00 p.m., sugar, rice and candles. It is *hora Peruana*, (Peruvian time) and after all that rush to get out, no one is in the law office yet. So, I'll go have a cup of coffee at Marta's Café and see how the day unfolds.

Green light, right turn and cobblestone clacking beneath my tires (clack, clack, clack), I drive up the narrow one-lane road toward the Plaza. Foot traffic is thick — like ants up and down crowded sidewalks, they move on either side of the narrow stone road on even narrower 20-inch wide sidewalks. Eyes stare at me behind the wheel with interest and curiosity; few women drive here. Turning the last corner before Plateros Street, I plead with the parking Genie to save me a space. Sure enough, right in front of the café' is a space big enough for our yellow Toyota truck. I check three times that the car is locked before I go into the café, briefcase in hand, for my first java of the day.

Marta greets me with her friendly gold-tooth smile and a kiss on the cheek. Sitting at her table we share light gossip over the Cusco style *café con leche* (Cusco latte). As we talk, the street noise and sounds of life increase around me. The day is on.

So many errands became a lot easier when CW received this second-hand truck in 1989 from the Peru Copper Mining CO (American company) in Lima. This donation came because of a meeting with the

Mining Co. Board of Directors after an introduction from my friend Cati, whom I met in 1987. She invited me into her home anytime I had CW work to do in Lima and even drove me around the unfamiliar streets the first year.

CHAPTER 9

Not All was Joyful

"…to make a difference, we must not ignore the small daily differences we can make which, over time, add up to big differences." — Marian Wright Edelman

Active Tuberculosis in the Children — 1988

AN RN FOR almost 40 years didn't prepare me to recognize the endemic Tuberculosis I was now experiencing. I took all the children to Antonio Loreno Hospital in Cusco for a medical work-up including a chest X-ray and discovered there was a shortage of film to do a chest X-ray and only available in tiny 3" x 4" pieces. There were shortages of everything, and clearly this was not what I was used to finding at my medical center. I vowed that on my next trip home I would collect some of the items needed to diagnose and treat the people in need here.

It was discovered that Ronald, Antonio and Fernando all had TB and needed to be treated. Roma, a friendly social worker, was there that first day at the hospital, and I was grateful for her help navigating through the indifference toward my group of children and getting the evaluation and treatment needed for some of the five kids I had in tow. Roma became an important contact and friend and was very helpful over the years. She was also the social worker who asked me to accept two girls in CW.

The children alerted the nurse in me, setting off an inner alarm that they needed more attention and a complete evaluation NOW. TB was endemic in Cusco and mostly ravaged the poor and malnourished. I was horrified with the attitude of the MD's and their non-treatment recommendations of more exercises to help Antonio. His untreated TB since childhood has severely damaged his normal childhood growth and development. Antonio clearly had pressure on his spinal cord and time was of the essence to get him treatment before he was unable to use his lower extremities. I was frustrated with the lack of medical care in Cusco and had nowhere to turn for the type of help he needed. It was then I remembered that I was given a piece of paper from a nurse colleague at my medical center in California with the name of a nursing school friend who entered the-convent upon graduation and happened to be running a health clinic in Arequipa, Peru, only one hour away by plane.

I called the clinic immediately. Sister Christina answered, and after listening to my fear for Antonio she told me to bring him ASAP and she would meet me at the airport in Arequipa. She told me not to worry; she would arrange for a bed with the Brothers who run the 'San Juan de Dios Hospital' for the poor. Slightly relieved, I told a 10-year-old Antonio of the need for us to go immediately. He understood and agreed.

The stairs we had to climb to enter the plane created a problem for him, and I was about to ask for help when two kind local businessmen stepped forward to lift him up the stairs. His first plane experience was a smooth and short one. The same businessmen helped us descend the stairs at our destination and we thanked them. Arequipa was a tiny airport and cars lined up waiting to pick up passengers on the edge of the tarmac. I searched for a nun in the normal full habit, the only kind of nun in Peru in 1988. Instead, I saw a woman in jeans and a plaid shirt waving at me as we descended the stairs of the plane. Sister Christina was a progressive Mercy sister from California and greeted us with a welcome smile and opened the door to her VW bug. Antonio and I climbed into the bug with only a small bag of personal items for each of us.

We drove directly to 'San Juan de Dios' where Antonio was admitted to the hospital and advised he would see the doctor presently and be told the plan of his care and that the Sisters would see to his toiletries and personal needs after I leave to return to the shelter in Cusco. I assured Antonio I would wait until the treatment plan was laid out before returning to Cusco. He was brave and trusted the Sisters; he too seemed relieved. Sister Christina and I left for the convent where I was invited to stay with the nuns while Antonio settled in.

I felt that he was finally in good hands and I could breathe normally again. I would be in touch by phone for much of the time he was there with a visit or two depending on his progress. They told me that he would be with them for about a year to treat his advanced condition. The Sisters were all nurses and over dinner they assured me they would be in constant contact with the brothers and the doctors regarding his prognosis and care. On the flight home, I felt we had barely escaped a serious tragedy and was grateful for the contacts that suddenly appeared when we needed them. I don't believe there are any accidents in life and being given the name of Sister Christina from my nursing colleague in California was synchronistic.

Rescuing Young Elena

While roaming the night streets looking for young children with a local volunteer, we spotted a young girl working with her drunken mother, and my stomach turned. Sofia, the local woman volunteer, spoke to her in Quechua and pleaded with her to let her daughter live in the shelter and go to school. The mother refused, unconcerned for her daughter's safety. Night after night, we found them just off on a side street and finally the drunk mother said okay. We took her home about midnight and got Elena settled into a bed when her mom banged on our door complaining we stole her daughter. Sofia and I went with the mother to the police station to make sure no report was made, and she agreed to let her daughter stay at CW. Now, it was of record by the mother. However, we had many visits late at night by this drunken mother and had to repeat the entire police visit. Her daughter always refused to go with her mother.

Not All Volunteers are Equal — 1988

The financial ups and downs of the early years were very hard in many ways. I went through so many volunteers who came only to steal what I brought from California for the shelter, and others who really didn't believe in our mission or value the children living on the streets. I weeded them out often, and I found myself alone too often after Phil moved on. I didn't see it coming, but the loneliness of this sort of project until it gets strong really risks its success.

Parents of the Street Children

Of the children who have lived for an extended period of time in the Shelter, we mostly knew no other members of their family, with the exception of maybe a brother they would bring to the shelter.

On a few rare occasions, a mother would show up at our door to see their son or daughter — to see where they lived or because the mother needed something.

One mother appeared at 7:00 a.m. one morning unannounced after her son had been with us for several years. She stayed about an hour and spoke privately with her son and he then called me to introduce his mother to his other mother, which surprised me — neither showed any discomfort with this introduction. She was pregnant again. Her son was genuinely touched that she made the trip from her far-away village to see him — most likely traveling day and night, which is why she arrived so early.

One of our girls who was about 11 years old lived with us in Cusco and relocated to Urubamba with the CW family. She was rescued and sent to us by a priest in the jungle who rescued her at about eight years old in an unsafe situation. Her mother was a prostitute and would have drunk men in her bed, along with her daughter nearby, and in extreme danger of a violation. At CW, she and another girl shared a bed on the girls' third floor and in Urubamba. She was in school with the other children in Urubamba, was progressing well and playing happily with the other girls. One day out of the blue at 6:00 a.m., there was loud banging on the front door of Urubamba house. It was a man with a document from the judge to take the girl at that moment to her mother, in the jungle. She was ripped away with only the clothes on her back and didn't even get to say goodbye to the other girls, and the adults who cared about her at CW were still asleep. It happened so fast. Fortunately, she communicates with us regularly, is married happily and has two children today, and has stayed in contact with us as she got older and has returned to CW Cusco needing medical attention at times, and Ruth provided that help. Like many of early children we occasionally text on Face Book.

Many stories I include in this book of the history of Chicuchas Wasi years have brought laughter and joy to all the participants of the CW family as we are now known. I have added a few of the more difficult stories anonymously to provide a sense of reality and the true balance of the CW life serving hundreds of children over 31 years. We hear from the adult Shelter kids fairly often; Lucho is married with three kids he is sending to school and owns an auto repair business, he came to visit me proudly one day so I could meet his three children; another has a restaurant business that is doing well in the valley; one owns and operates a successful bar; and yet another is married with three kids and his own taxi business. Those we connect with that have children are educating them and are responsible fathers and mothers today.

Three kids from the earlier years of the CW family, have graduated from College: Hipolito in Business Economy and is married with

three daughters. Efrain graduated from College and is an award win-
ning tour guide and Tour Business owner, is married and father of
three children. Rosa graduated from College a professional registered
Nurse and the mother of a one–year–old son. We are so proud of you
our shinning stars.

CHAPTER 10

What We Focus on is What We Will Create

"Listen to the wind, it talks.
Listen to the silence, it speaks.
Listen to your heart, it knows."
— Native American Proverb

Attitude and Focus Means Everything!

THE FIRST TWO years of CW were more than I expected, demanding more of me than I believed I had to give and skills I had yet to learn. The few local friends and supporters of the shelter were not always who they represented themselves to be and had personal interests. My experience in life did not prepare me for the reality I witnessed; the abandoned kids who lived on the streets of Cusco city were invisible to most, who looked away; it hurt to see the indifference toward the many children, some with young siblings as young as five or six years old, who survived by their wits, suffered hypothermia and died of neglect here. These kids won my heart; they found joy in the smallest things and would join their voices in a song with gusto at any given moment. They knew terrible loss and pain and learned they could step over it all for a few minutes and lift us all. My personal childhood as described in the introduction evolved around a serious fierce work-ethic and the family business — though it gave me the life of middle-class Californian — was not much fun, easy or flush with money, but we had enough; yet we rarely found the simple joy together that I discovered these children could muster.

Personal Crisis - and Growth

While reading my personal journals from 1987 and 1988, I am shocked to see how depressed I was over the start-up years of Chicuchas Wasi in Cusco. Overwhelmed and burned out, I was at a loss how to raise the funds we needed. I was committed to fundraise to support the emergency shelter that Phil and I opened with Ronald, and soon after added three more children in need of a safe place to sleep at night. Flying back and forth from Cusco to California to raise funds by selling folk art, earrings, and textiles and asking for donations and supplies was both exhilarating and exhausting. Somehow, I managed to raise enough to keep us afloat; it was literally hand-to-mouth.

My Australian friend, Phil, and I met in '86 while we both lived in Cusco. We would meet weekly over lemon pie; or if an especially tough week something stronger, to ramble in ENGLISH our joys and frustrations with the cultural obstacles we encountered personally in Peru, with our skimpy Spanish. Phil cared about the kids who followed us around and responded with an immediate YES when I asked him to return in 1987 to help get the CW Shelter set up. He stayed 10 months and was a big help most of that first year. Living with a bunch of independent and unruly kids was not a good fit for him. But he stuck it out physically and was an enormous help to comply with all of the bureaucratic Peruvian requirements. I cannot imagine being alone that year with all the red tape and rubber stamps and stamping for every legal document. Phil and I plowed through these early months and both laughed and cried in frustration at times. Emotionally, I still felt alone under the weight of the many hats I had agreed to wear. Fundraising was the biggest and worst on the long list required to provide for the children and legally create a nonprofit in Peru. For me, living with mostly boys initially seemed like a continuation of raising my own three California sons more or less; my birth sons would not last one night in the reality these kids dealt with, and so it was not as difficult for me. I like children, and these kids became my teachers and guides to help me understand how I could make a difference in their reality and culture.

Meanwhile, the personal crisis of my inner and outer world continued to collide, and slowly I began to plant my feet solidly on the ground and deepen the spiritual connection that was behind the re-creation of a new me — or, better said, waking up the true me.

The reality of creating an emergency shelter for abandoned children revealed quickly how lacking I was / we were. No experience! Little money! Phil and I were in this same boat and we were frantically bailing water. We pushed ahead and opened the shelter, and to keep things moving we busied ourselves buying the basics like more beds and sheets. Phil and I were both struggling with the impotence we felt, not knowing where and how to begin to help these kids. So, we sat down, put our heads together, got serious and went to work to divide up the plan. Meanwhile, more kids entered the shelter — some stayed and went to school, washed their bodies and clothes and honored the rules (no stealing, lying or hoarding food), but others preferred the freedom of the street without any rules; the revolving door of CW Shelter.

Local University students and other volunteers came off and on to help. As mentioned earlier, some volunteers had other intentions and stole from us all they could. We learned to discern more carefully and weed out the ones who didn't fit. Being foreigners was a magnet to attract the wrong people, interested in enriching themselves— often a painful betrayal.

As I tip-toed through the ups and downs of my loneliness and waded through the people I attracted who thought they could fill my days and their pockets, only too quickly I learned — well, not that quickly — that mostly their energy was not what I needed, and it pulled me farther away from who I truly am, yet I didn't see it at first. Only when I crashed and burned emotionally, sending me back to my daily meditations and to the source that gives me strength, courage and clarity, did I get it. I finally surrendered to this loving and powerful energy that held me in its embrace and I found me again.

By recognizing the judgments that had seeped into my thoughts, I eventually changed my attitude and my limited view, opening new doors and windows for change. With a new, more positive attitude came new opportunity and the growth to success. As soon as I did this, I realized with fresh new awareness that I didn't need anyone to fulfill me or bring me the joy and love I hungered for. I surrendered completely, and my life and nonprofit changed. Sincere new people came to lend a hand. We filled the house with love together.

My earlier judgments were harsh, and I often misunderstood the extreme poverty and resulting dysfunction by which I was surrounded. When my attitude changed, so did my reality. What we think, speak and imagine is what we will draw to us — magnetically. I was more positive; attracted more of what I wanted for the kids. And yes, I still worked hard, but had growing support as CW slowly attracted others of like mind.

New Doors Open

I was invited to a Nursing conference for English-speaking nurses working in Peru sponsored by the US Embassy where I met new Lima friends and through them good fundraising ideas and contacts. The workshop was full of people like me doing near impossible projects like CW. Most were religious, but not all. I met a few others with similar interests and some who not only thought like me, they put it into action. With so many like-minded new connections, the loneliness just evaporated. Their stories empowered me, lifted my spirits and let me see how my attitude needed to change. It did, and I did, and the struggle lifted.

The American Chamber of Commerce Director of Lima was introduced to me with amazing possibilities. The door swung wide open. I was raising funds while still in Peru, instead of writing/mailing out tons of grant proposals that no one read or responded to, and not running back and forth from California and Cusco, Peru. We were donated a yellow pickup from Peru Mining CO in 1988. The American Chamber of Commerce hosted a golf tournament and raised $20K for the CW shelter in Cusco. UNICEF of Lima agreed to fund a five-day workshop by CW in Cusco to bring all the groups working to aid the street kids together. We put our heads together to share our successes and failures; good caring people showed up who were not indifferent and did not avert their eyes away from the suffering kids. More than 80 participants came together, and we developed relationships and shared stories that were profoundly helpful.

After that, I made frequent trips to Lima to fundraise with my new list of contacts. Somehow, I convinced Lima Toyota in 1990 to donate a shiny new red 4x4 double cab pick-up to CW; Goodyear committed to keeping us in tires as needed in Cusco; a Peruvian company donated a kitchen stove and so much more.

It was during this period that a young Andean woman, Ruth Uribe, born, raised and educated as a teacher in Cusco connected with Chicuchas Wasi at the 4day workshop, 'Survival of the Street Child in Cusco' in Cusco that we sponsored and UNICEF funded. I instantly observed that Ruth was a passionate and like-minded woman who knew and loved these kids as I did. She demonstrated her generosity and altruism early in life as a volunteer at the church free meal program and knew most of the street kids we served. Initially she became an occasional volunteer on weekends and little by little become more. From now on you will read much more about Ruth and what she brought to the children and Chicuchas Wasi going forward.

She knew her people and was quick to spot the insincere ones. She showed her leadership skills right away, her commitment, and eventually became my right arm and discovered that CW was her passion too.

Sanctuary in Rumichaka

Hard moments and Self Discovery

> *"And never forget, no matter how overwhelming life's*
> *challenges and problems seem to be that one person*
> *can make a difference in the world. In fact, it is always*
> *because of one person that all the changes that matter in*
> *the world come about. So be that one person."*
> — R. Buckminster Fuller

Thousands of abandoned teens and younger children roamed the Cusco back streets and slept at night in doorways, and under market tables, with only few safe shelters available in 1988. And try as I did, I was unable to grasp this reality I would witness daily and especially at night when the kids came out to work, steal or worse. The local population just didn't see them. These children were my first friends in Cusco, stealing from me initially before realizing I was staying and then began to trust and protect me. My trips to the market to buy food essentials for the day's soup would usually have two or three of these kids at my side, mostly to protect me from the older thieves they all knew and learned from. Protecting me from these thieves often resulted in harm to them — they would be beat up later by the ones who wanted to rob me, whom they prevented.

I learned about real poverty my first year in Cusco and Lima, and still have trouble with the injustice of it all. No social services are available and little children are left to sleep in the piles of other children to ward of the cold and hypothermia at night. Most of their food is stolen or they go hungry. Tourists gave them money; sadly, it is used for pinball, glue to sniff or other drugs. Some kind tourists buy them food to eat, and this is better. Some tourists invite them to eat with them, ignoring the nasty looks of the restaurant owners, and listen to the made-up sad story of the moment the children have learned to deliver to survive. New shoes, jackets and other clothing items are gifted to them, initially by me as well, until I saw them for sale on a corner to get money for pinball, food or drugs.

So raw and hard was this reality that it deeply challenged my moral beliefs from my own childhood. I didn't want to believe what I saw, or that many of these children just died of neglect. At times I was unable to manage my emotions and would fall into despair, constantly asking myself, "Why am I here trying to make a difference against overwhelming indifference?"

One day my friend Beverly invited me to her home deeper in the rural sacred valley. An expat like myself, she recognized my anguish and offered me the space to calm down to have a better handle of my role here, my deep desire to make a difference. How I might do this?

I packed my daypack and headed to Beverly's home as cargo in the back of a pick-up truck, unsure if I could hold my emotions a minute longer. Once there, I hiked down to the river alone with an apple for lunch and just sat quietly with the birds and sounds of the river. This gave me the private space I needed. I cried and cried. I slept, and I meditated until I felt lighter and no longer alone. This was what I needed so much. I began to change my understanding of bigger reality and the value of my small part to make a difference and my attitude about how it was so impossible. I recalled this quote:

> "Never doubt that a small group of thoughtful,
> committed citizens can change the world. Indeed, it is
> the only thing that ever has." — Margaret Mead

I returned to Beverly's home refreshed to help prepare and share a meal, a glass of wine and listen to her play her guitar and laugh together over the strange and unpredictable lives we live.

When My Attitude Changed, Everything Changed. YES, EVERYTHING!

Chicuchas Wasi put on a 4-day Conference with UNICEF called "Survival of the Street Child in Cusco" — 1988

Many came, but Ruth stood out. The young, bronze-skinned, black-eyed beauty with the gleaming long, black hair that framed a gorgeous face sat eyes focused on the speakers. During short group interactions, she spoke with conviction and experience. She was on my team for the 'hands-on' street experience late that night. The children sleeping under tables in the market knew her and clearly trusted her. Later she showed up to help in the CW Shelter on weekends, to knead bread dough with five or six pairs of eager little hands and toss flour-coated food on the table, floor and clothes, turning them to a powdery white. Big toothy smiles shined out of brown faces dusted in flour. We all laughed till we cried; kneaded, baked and ate the warm tender bread we made. Those moments bonded us forever with mutual understanding of something not yet shared with words. The CW heart knew.

She came and went, faithful to her studies and later her job as a student teacher. After graduation, her work in Pisac all week meant we had her only on weekends. We all worked hard, laughed, and felt love everywhere filling empty hearts, beating faster than we could fill.

I remember the Christmas crazies of one annual Chocolatada event. Since the CW beginning, we recognized the value of showing our resident kids how kindness and generosity to others less fortunate could feel good and make everyone feel good and be happy. We created the CW annual Christmas outreach program where our resident kids would deliver the traditional Christmas hot chocolate and pannetone sweet bread party for less fortunate kids. University students volunteered enthusiastically to help make this happen. We needed many things and a location bigger than our house we learned the prior year. *"I'll borrow two big pots,"* Ruth offered at the planning meeting. *"The milk and chocolate are donated, and so is the flour,"* I joined in. *"We need fruit pieces and toys,"* added another student volunteer. *"I can work on that if you organize the kids,"* I volunteered.

"Done!" Heads all nodded together and Excitement filled CWs small dining room, our impromptu meeting hall.

With little money and lots of enthusiasm, we planned the party. We could expect many to come, more than 250+ this year. Our resident kids were excited to put on this party for other children less fortunate, and they made tickets to hand out to them.

"We'd better not have it here at the Shelter." I said. The neighbors haven't recovered from the 200 kids at our door and clogging the entry hall to their apartments last year. I remember we used to play "ding-dong garbage can" when I was a kid. You lean a garbage can up against the door, ring the bell, and run. When the door opens, the garbage spills out around their feet — kids are kids everywhere. The Andean version was to ring doorbells and run. Thank God, there was no garbage handy. Suffice to say, the neighbors don't talk to us anymore.

"We can use the University Patio on the Plaza," suggested a university student volunteer.

"I have a friend who can fix it," says another.

We received 900 kids or so that Christmas; the gifts of toys ran out, and so did the hot chocolate and sweet bread with fruit pieces in it, but songs were sung by all and games were played. Our resident kids were filled with a special warmth from giving to other street kids, noted by the looks on their faces as they poured the hot chocolate carefully balancing the cup for the little ones, surely thinking of younger brothers and sisters absent.

Somehow the hard work never seemed to feel like work — more like fun — and we planted seeds all over that day. I will never see most of the trees, but I'm sure most took and grew tall. Ruth and I were both moved deeply and connected with our first shared vision of this commitment. Like modern day nuns, almost, we trusted that the way and the form would be shown to us. Others wanted to see the form in dollars. Well two out of five is not too bad. Reflecting back, the way has always been shown to us and the funds have always appeared when needed, albeit sometimes in the midst of unpleasant stress levels.

CHAPTER 11

Visiting Antonio in Arequipa

"Sharing with one another and blessing one another embodies the spirit of generosity and compassion. Like a tiny first spark, it is the original gift of creation. So, light a candle, and know that your inner spirit burns bright and glorious. Let it be seen and offer your light to one another." — Grandma Moses

FIVE MONTHS FLEW by with everyone in school and the normal activities of our busy CW Shelter family and positive reports about Antonio and his treatment were ongoing. We all missed him, and were all thinking of Antonio alone in the hospital the last five months, and it occurred to me to take an adventurous train trip with all the kids to visit him.

I talked this idea over with volunteers and some local friends who advised me not to take local children to Arequipa alone without Peruvian adults with me. A train was a 12-hour **slow** ride, but incredibly scenic of the Andean countryside. These were difficult times in Peru, politically, but also with child trafficking, so I heeded their warnings and we all went on an adventure with a local family to keep me safe.

The children loved the train, even though they were four kids per seat in two-seat rows. The family took up another two rows. We packed blankets, food and water, and all food was gone about half-way. Peruvian trains stop every few hours for the local people to come aboard with incredible roasted lamb and potatoes, hot coffee and packaged junk food for sale, and we bought a little of everything. I learned to sit far away from the one bathroom on our train car, as it would get a lot of *over*-use in 12 hours.

We arrived in Arequipa and were all were excited to be visiting Antonio and this newer and more modern city than Cusco. I was stopped by a stern Peruvian couple on the street and asked why I had so many children with me. Fortunately, the family with me stepped up to answer them about their children. At the hospital, one of the nuns took us to a building next to the hospital that had simple dorm rooms and bathrooms with showers, but no frills like soap. We were told these accommodations were for families visiting the children in the hospital and for us to make ourselves comfortable. This was perfect since our budget didn't include a hotel for us all.

The Sister nurse caring for Antonio told us that he could stay with us in the dorm and sleep there with the other kids. The young boys were happy to be close to their buddy again. Antonio had received spinal surgery to fuse the spine where the TB had caused damage and was now in a full body cast — armpit to thigh. I noticed that it looked like he had lost weight because the cast was loose. The Sister confirmed it was about time to change the cast.

These were mountain children and so was the family traveling with us, none of whom have seen the ocean or visited it ever. We were only a two-hour bus ride from the coast, and it seemed a waste not to let them all have an hour or so to experience the beach and ocean. I should have realized that in this group of 13, I was the only one who knew how to swim, and I felt the bite of stress until we left the ocean. The cost of the bus ride to the coast was minimal since children go at half-fare or less, and it was too good to pass up. The oohs and aahs from inside the bus when the huge ocean came into view was pretty wonderful for us all. I was so glad we took this opportunity that would be unlikely to happen again for them for many years, if at all. The Nurse Sister smiled at me when I asked if we could take Antonio with us, and told us not to get the cast wet, smiling. I mentioned we would be careful, but that his cast needed changing anyway. She waved us off, and this was definitely off the record. No papers were signed, and I doubt she told anyone that she gave us permission to take Antonio to the coast.

Our adventure to Arequipa City and then Ica City on the Coast was not planned as a fun trip, but it seemed right to bring a little joy to all when you think of the lives they have led up to now. We returned late that night to Arequipa and everyone slept on the bus. The next day we began our long train ride back to Cusco and school assignments to be made up.

Cusco was wonderful to come back to, familiar and cozy in our little shelter. We cooked a hearty soup and bought some bread, and everyone crashed into bed and slept well. That night I got a call from Sister Christina to warn me that the hospital had an outbreak of chicken pox just after we left. My mind had visions of all the kids in close contact playing together and I groaned. Yep, everyone got chicken pox, which I treated with watered-down oatmeal smeared over their bodies, then stuffed some of them in my long johns so the oatmeal plastered over their bodies would stay in place and we got through it.

Our routine went back to normal the next day and you could feel how content we all were. Meanwhile, Ronald and Fernando were both in the treatment for tuberculosis at that time, with weekly injections of Streptomycin that I administered in the shelter over six months — a treatment outdated in developed countries by then in favor of a shorter multiple drug therapy that was not available in Peru.

Early Creative Fundraising

Struggling to keep the CW shelter open and food on the table for the 12 plus resident children required adult supervision, food supplies and a budget that was always big challenge. As CW founder, it had turned out that I was still THE fundraiser. Constant brainstorming for new ideas and more creative out-of-the box type of fundraising is needed going forward. OK! So, what does that look like?

In Cusco I bought Peruvian Folk Art (earrings, bracelets, textiles and miscellaneous small items) to carry to California and sell at small gatherings to raise money for the shelter. A talented board member made earring boards to display them for us. I hauled them everywhere full of earrings — to my Medical facility, grocery store, and post office parking lot and other public places where I knew I would run into friends and neighbors, and people bought them. A lot of the Folk Art was sold this way, even out of my car to friends I met at the post office. Remember the old story of *'a wandering man in an overcoat and who opens his coat to reveal about 50 watches stuck to the inner lining for sale'* — that was me. I felt like a part of that old joke about creative enterprise. But I used those earring boards and that was how I sold earrings everywhere the first years. I was never without them: $15 here and $15 there, and it all added up. The CW board still laughs at the reality that we still have about 300 pairs from the 1980s. That fact puts a smile on the five founding board members who also sold them anywhere they could. Earrings just seem to materialize when we thought we had sold most of them, like the loaves and fishes. We did CW slide presentations in California, raising more funds toward our $15,000-$20,000 budget of the early years. But the trips to California to raise money were more difficult that first year when it was just Phil and I in Cusco, and I was needed hands-on at the shelter to help Phil with the kids. Somehow, we did it.

Time for NEW More CREATIVE Fundraising

The amount of money I was raising with Folk-Art was like filling a bathtub a drop at a time. I needed to raise larger amounts and faster without leaving the shelter. A Peruvian travel agent in Cusco and a member of our CW Cusco Board of Directors taught me how I could use trips to California to organize tours to Cusco and raise a lot more for the CW Shelter. Thanks to his guidance and management of the Cusco portion of the tour, I began to lead groups to Cusco and raised a good portion of the operating budget for the year. CW was onto something — '**Opening the Heart** — A Spiritual Journey to Machu Picchu -TOURS.' We created *'Visit Machu Picchu'* tour flyers to lead tours to Machu Picchu and Cusco. Over the years I led many tours, and still do today 30 years later at times. All of my groups visited the early CW Shelter, and today in 2018 tourists visit our CW School for Girls often.

The first 1990 travelers were mostly CW board members and friends from home. Everyone enjoyed the trip, and all laughed, ate and danced with the children one evening. Georgia, a professional artist on the tour, painted a mural of the CW children on our Cusco dining room wall that held up for seven to eight years.

Efrain, a 30-year member of the CW family and one of our own early shelter boys, is a husband and responsible father of three today. He owns his own Apex Peru Adventure travel company and is an active CW Cusco board member who takes over the tour groups I send or bring with me. (But I am jumping ahead a few years.) Creative fundraising was definitely a lot more fun and the best way to fundraise and keep my sanity.

CHAPTER **12**

CW Moves to Urubamba in 1990

"Your time is limited, so don't waste it living someone else's life. Don't be trapped by dogma — which is living with the results of other people's thinking. Don't let the noise of others' opinions drown out your own inner voice. And most important, have the courage to follow your heart and intuition. They somehow already know what you truly want to become. Everything else is secondary." — Steve Jobs commencement speech after cancer diagnosis

AT FIRST GLANCE, the big old house in Urubamba was a great idea with the potential for a business to support the CW Shelter. However, when I reflect on the challenge then of buying it for us all to live in, and also use as a fundraising business, it presented both positives and negatives. I am an optimist, so just didn't focus on the obstacles and they went away. **Creative** is my NEW magic word for CW fundraising since the usual form for a nonprofit to raise money was near impossible in Urubamba or Cusco.

The California Board of Directors didn't embrace the B&B idea or the travel tours to Cusco that I could lead with a local tour guide and friend. They feared the liability that they could face if there was an accident. Since I was living in Peru and saw the reality we faced with different glasses, I decided that I, as a person (not CW), could both lead tours and run the B&B and not put the Board at risk. The idea was so good and the property I found so perfect for the B&B idea I decided to do both as Rae Lewis, not as Founder of CW. However, I did have to buy the property, and with liquidated personal funds and family financial help I did, and did not involve the nonprofit. Now, I also needed to be at the property most of the time since I was the only English speaker for the tourists who came. Unless I was leading a tour, I would not be returning to California as often, so we could run the B&B. Informal as it was, it was fun, we all learned, and it really did support us those years.

The tours were also fun and raised funds much more quickly and reliably than the dreaded grant writing while I was living in Peru.

The kids understood we found a way to support us all and jumped in to help. We had work to do to prepare for B&B guests. Our first vehicle, a second-hand yellow truck, made many trips to the nearby river to collect river rocks for paths around the grounds. We literally wore out the bed of the truck on these trips. Anywhere we went the truck and cab were full of material to fix up our new business. Rolling down the mountain road from Cusco to Urubamba required more entertainment, and soon the kids were belting out songs popular here in the mountains. Inside the double cab the rest of us joined in and we had a chorus of joy. Hard to believe that these were the same kids we rescued off the streets and from the abuse and exploitation. What teachers they were for us adults. The kids went to school weekdays while I sewed curtains for the guest rooms, and on weekends we all worked hard to ready the rooms and fix the plumbing for our soon-to-arrive clients. By nightfall we were all thinking of sleep. I would wake some mornings to uncontrollable giant body-gripping yawns taking over my body that would squeeze my eyes like a damp sponge until drops fell onto my cheeks. Like waves they came stretching my mouth as wide as it is possible to open. This is waking up for me in Urubamba. Sleep is so deep and coma-like I must have serious 02 hunger when I wake.

The Urubamba property was a challenge, yes, but a heck of a lot of fun for all of us. We all worked hard getting it ready and seeing the mess we made of ourselves and looking at each other, we all laughed our heads off. We painted the building and a local artist created a large ceramic logo, 'Urpi Wasi' over a globe and 'House of Peace' below it, and placed it on the main wall facing the street side of the building. We collected river rocks along the nearby river in our truck to create paths around the house and pool. Did I mention there was a swimming pool at this property? And I was the only person who knew how to swim. What was I thinking? Mountain people mostly do not swim. So, the first thing we urgently needed to focus on was swimming lessons for all kids and staff alike. Since our kids were fearless, we started off with a race from the deep end to the shallow end doing the dog paddle stroke. In no time we had about 15 fish swimming, more or less, and able to keep themselves from drowning.

The big old house was made of adobes and had two floors and staircases that went all over — staircase to the main dining room, staircase to the guest rooms, staircase to the CW Shelter wing and back stairs to everything. We cultivated the two acres of the rich soil of the property with cabbage, potatoes, corn, squash and others. The entire property was surrounded by a six-foot-tall adobe wall 11 inches thick and kept us all safe and secure at night. We hired Maestro Juan, a born farmer and a recommended security man, to manage the main door. In no time he captured the spirit of the CW family and became part of all our activities. He contributed great ideas and had the boys involved in some learning repair activities. So, a lot of hands-on learning was going on for us all.

One day in 1990 while I was preparing food in the upstairs B&B kitchen (as opposed to our private rammed earth FAGUN in our corner downstairs private area kitchen), I looked out the window into our field and noticed Maestro Juan driving a huge cow or ox over the field — plowing it to make it ready to plant. I asked him where he got the animal? He smiled and said he borrowed it from a friend. The local Andean farmers all share a lot, including their labor to co-op build a home or harvest a field. Anything that needed fixing from plumbing, like when a small frog got stuck coming out of the faucet of the bathroom sink, to an electric power break in the lines Juan repaired. He fixed a leaky roof; he took over the painting, not happy with the boys' and Ruth and my results, and produced food for our table. Maestro Juan was part of the family. He ate with us, celebrated birthdays with us, and watched English video movies with us over popcorn and hot tea. No one treated a peasant employee like family in Peru I learned, but he was part of the CW family to us. There was not much happening in this village after sunset, so we made our own fun.

Getting Ready for Business

The political unrest of the '80s brought broken windows, shouting, tear gas and loud car bombs exploding too often in Cusco. The constant visual of police in riot gear provided a good reason to relocate Chicuchas Wasi and the core street kids ripe for recruiting by terrorists, to the safer Sacred Valley.

We loaded the big hired Mac truck with bunkbeds, dressers, a refrigerator, tables, books, and chairs, piled up like the Beverly Hillbillies and headed to our new home one hour outside of Cusco, to Urubamba in the Sacred Valley — all 14 of us by then.

Over the next month we scrubbed, nailed, painted, weeded, and secured doors to our two-acre compound. Groaning under the load, our yellow Toyota pick-up hauled more loads of rock from the river than I can count. These river rocks formed the cypress tree-lined walkways and trails around the house we now lived in.

Inspired by our developing B&B business plan, 13 heads brainstormed together how we could attract clients, and our new creative ideas started flowing. Everyone in the Urubamba CW family now had a vested interest in earning our living.

Standard big adobes are perfect for a simple sauna we all agreed, and our young entertainers and Maestro Juan happily got busy stomping with their dancing feet smashing into piles of mud and straw to make enough adobes for an Andean Sauna. Maestro Juan found an old oil drum and recycled it into a perfect wood-burning stove for sauna heat and steam. Wooden bench seats lined the inner walls, and eucalyptus leaves were added to boiling water to promote healthy lungs. It was ready, and we all tried it out. This became an effective cure for any cold or just to relax. The sauna was a treat for the CW family, plus we had paying local customers who came just for the sauna or for tourists who stayed at the B&B and used the sauna.

CW was open for business, offering accommodations for weary travelers in our newly created 'California-style B&B' we named "URPI WASI," meaning the House of Peace. The CW style of creative fundraising involving locals and foreigners put food on the table. It so happened there was very little available for travelers needing a place to rest in Urubamba at that time, so a perfect source of funding for CW and a good fit for visitors.

Ruth, 23, lived at home in Cusco and was a kindergarten teacher in Pisac. An active weekend volunteer in the Cusco Shelter, she came to the new CW home in Urubamba to help out every weekend and then returned to her family in Cusco. She brought an understanding and a passion to work with the CW kids full-time but was torn by local restriction born of custom: Women leave home to marry or enter the convent — not before. Ruth was destined to co-lead the future of CW and to be hands-on with us. Step by step, little by little, she and I took turns persuading her mother of the virtues and honor of our work, and that she would be safe with us. With one daughter already in the convent, Carlota wasn't eager to see another daughter avoid marriage, grandchildren and security. Months went by. Tears and words spent, Ruth moved in. Fixing up her room, she had 13 eager helpers thrilled to have her join our family team. Her mother relaxed, became a frequent visitor, and began to see her daughter with new eyes.

Ruth, hiding behind dark sunglasses, jumped in and tackled new male-dominated experiences bravely — like the time we added a wing to the house with an additional five rooms. She and I were the contractors giving direction to the subcontractors, much to the bug-eyed horror of these Andean men — chained by custom that macho men could not work for women, they initially refused to work for us. Well, these women had the money! And that seemed to soften the old custom. Ruth and I silently divided the responsibility with eye contact and Ruth climbed into the cab of the big tractor truck with its driver as 12 thrilled ogling men, who immediately fell in love with Ruth, climbed in the truck bed. We hired the men from the Urubamba market to collect and load our new 5500 adobes still all scattered on small farms nearby and then unload them all at our new home 'Urpi Wasi' (House of Peace). The CW boys and I drove our brick-loaded small truck to the back of our property to unburden the complaining saggy tires. The 23 freshly-made beds of our B&B were ready for customers and Carmen, our newly recruited cook extraordinaire, was busy preparing the lunch meal for our return. We had to feed the men also, so a big pot of soup was being prepared for us all.

Triumphant, Ruth returned filthy with clay earth covered black hair and powdery grimy yellow colored skin with black eyes popping out of the center. The less-than-pleased, now openly disgruntled, men unloaded the adobes and formed a line behind her to collect their wages — from a woman. Alone later, we smiled and slapped a High 5, knowing we'd killed another dragon.

I watched Ruth go from unsure and afraid, to experienced and in control when challenged to the max by male authority figures. Her eyes would shine like black bullets of determination and no nonsense with this group of men she made actually do some work, and she won. Celebrations of popcorn, Anise herbal tea, and laughter filled our nights.

Exhausted but happy with our success, the kids finally in bed, and our work finished, we could plan the 5:00 a.m. breakfast. "Urpi Wasi" was full; a group of 24 tourists from California required one more bed to accept the group, but we only had 23. We learned to accommodate tourists by shuffling a bit. It was Ruth's turn to loan her bed this time, and I had the biggest bed, so we girls had to triple or double-up when needed to accommodate a large group. We were tired, but still shared stories and secrets late into the night. We had become a trusted family of 13-15 kids, Carmen the cook, Maestro Juan our all-round handyman and security, and Ruth and I in leadership roles.

Ruth and I both felt called to this work and formed a sisterhood around the CW mission for the children of Cusco — one leader from California and one leader from Cusco who would co-create the CW future. Little did we know then, Ruth would marry a Cusco lawyer in love with CW as much as we were and often lend us a legal hand to help CW.

Efrain Valles M. — His 30 years with CW

When I was little, I always dreamed of great things even though I had nothing at the time. I was almost seven years old when I lost my father. After that, my mother took care my three brothers and me. During those years, terrorism was gaining more strengthen Peru and of course poverty and inflation made Peruvians' lives more and more difficult.

During these years of need I learned to survive with the sale of postcards, ceramics, textiles etc., but it did not take long until one day my mother had to leave for the capital (Lima) with my three brothers, and I would be left alone in Cusco. I believe this was the second challenge that life would place in my path, because the first was to learn to live with the absence of my father.

Many years passed in which I met many friends from the street and found places to eat and sleep until one day Rae, a tourist who came to visit Machu Picchu and then saw the poverty and need of the people, created a Peruvian Foundation, Chicuchas Wasi, for children and invited me to visit and spend the weekend in Urubamba. I really

113

loved that visit because the place was a dream — swimming pool, soccer field, green areas, and a large family that would take care of you... well it was the place where I would like to go constantly, but on that weekend, I was just a guest.

During the several months since I visited Chicuchas Wasi, I continued to sell my things in the main square of Cusco. I continued eating in a dining room where the nuns gave food to people in need and I was blessed to meet Ruth there who over the years would become a mother. I also continued to sleep in the dormitory for street children and of course I also continued attending my school and educating myself.

One day Rae invited me to spend another weekend at the Foundation as a reward for my good behavior and that would be the last invitation since I would stay to live and share my student life with 8 other children who were in the same situation as me. I was the most privileged child of a whole group of children ... I felt happy, I was happy.

For a few years I had 8 brothers and I would share all my joys and sorrows with them, I learned to dream more and live my life. I learned not to remember anything from the past and focus on a better future and so I did, because Rae who over the years with the love that I received from her became my other mother and gave me the tools and the guidance to develop in my time as a student of higher education. What a great privilege to have two mothers besides my biological mother.

Today, more than 20 years have gone by, I have 3 children and a beautiful wife by my side. I graduated as an official tour guide, and as far as possible I try to return what I received because I firmly believe that if they could make the change in someone like me, I can also do it with other girls from the Chicuchas Wasi Foundation that today educates more than 120 girls.

I learned in this short section of my life that there are no limits to our dreams when things are given and done from the heart, when you think big and believe that there is nothing impossible, perhaps *difficult — but never ever impossible. I learned that life gives you stumbling and sad moments as part of its lesson, but it is not so you collapse and fall, but rather so you learn to get up and start jogging, because you walked and stumbled and now it's time to jog.*

I learned that there are no limits to a dream and that above all, as a human being, I should always feel special, and to make this world special too.

Thanks forever, to Ruth and Rae my mothers forever, to my biological mother whom I love with all my heart and above all things to God for giving me the privilege of living this whole life.

"IF I WOULD NOT HAVE FALLEN AND COLLAPSED THOUSANDS OF TIMES, I WOULD NOT HAVE LEARNED THE PAIN OR THE WAY OF LIFTING ME 10 THOUSAND TIMES MORE" — EFRAIN VALLEYS M

Maestro Juan — 1990-1998

Maestro Juan was 35 and old already. Born a *'campesino'* (peasant); he spent most of those years working the family fields. He understood well the land, the plants, and the animals. He was gentle, hardworking and could barely read. Elena was his senior by at least 10 years with two sons when he married her, and they have two daughters and another son together. She had aged even faster than he. Every day she sold fruit that she bought from another vender in the market, spread out on a *'manta'* (blanket) on the ground by the entry gate in front of the Hospital *'Seguro'* (Social Insurance Hospital.) Her eldest daughter Marisol often helped her, and with the domestic chores of the family she often missed school.

Juan was a man of integrity. He was raised in extreme poverty but had been given a wealth of values. Juan came to me from a friend and was hired as our security doorman for the B&B to ward off unwanted curiosity seekers and drunks. Slowly he took control of the earth on our two acres he loved. He planted roses, and grafted 45 different ones in all around our Grotto for the Mother that he built out of stones with the children. Corn and potatoes grew alongside the little car park (the kids used as a little soccer field) and cabbage, carrots and onions in back along the wall marking the property line. Too many fruit trees to count were sprinkled around the two-acre parcel. There were apples, peaches, pears, lemon grapefruit, acapoli cherries (like elderberry), and we ate it all.

When the roof leaked, and we needed someone to fix it, Juan would say, *"Mamma — yo lo hago"* (mamma don't worry I'll fix it), and he did. He fixed broken windows when the kids played too hard. He fixed the bunkbeds when they started to fall down on each other when the green wood started to bend. He would lovingly care for our newly-arrived Red 4x4 truck and kept it shinning — frowning at me over a new bump or bruise to the wine-red color.

Slowly he became a male role model and support person in the project — a refuge for abandoned children, mostly boys. He was part of the family and he found projects around the grounds to do with the boys and taught them practical skills.

The Juan I met in 1990 who was silent unless spoken to, never lifting his eyes off the ground, had transformed into a man of many skills and of great value to me, and all of us, and he knew it. I depended on him for everything around the house. I would ask his advice about something I didn't understand and later he would offer his advice when the boys were up to something and thought I might not have noticed. He became my sidekick at times on the hour-long trips over the mountain during a difficult political time in Peru. He would delegate certain chores to the boys, grab his jacket and tell me, *"Mamma, I am going with you to Cusco."* (It was too late for me to go alone). His loyalty and affection for me brought tears to my eyes. He had found the courage to stand against his lifelong oppressors to protect me. I am honored to know Juan.

Evening Antics and Fun in Urubamba

One evening after dinner the 13 of us huddled around the TV, ready to watch a video for the third time — *The Thorn Birds*. I collected a box of VHS videos in California and hauled them back to Urubamba with me. This made us all happy since there were only two TV channels available in Urubamba and the Mayor picked what he liked — sports and soaps. The popcorn and anise tea were ready. The film was rolling. I sat on a chair while Ruth dyed my hair roots. Hipolito, our 15-year-old house poet, had very straight black hair, and this evening while watching the video he asked me to make his hair curly like mine. One look at his short black wires sticking straight up, and I smiled at the picture in my mind. *"Come on, Rae – por favor – si puedes, Rae,"* he pleaded. *"OK,"* I said, and out came the pink roller curlers I knew would do nothing for his hair but would be so entertaining for the rest of us. One by one as we watched the movie, I rolled up clumps of his hair into the pink rollers and clamped them. His hair still escaped around the corners and at the ends sticking straight out like black pipe cleaners in all directions — so normal in our crazy home that no one even teased him. Ruth and I held back the laughter, but the image was too funny for words! I took a photo to remind him one day.

Some evenings we had skits and all the boys (girls were being too adult) dressed in costume — Ruth's clothes mainly —and came in with some domestic funny antics from our family life. Next came the romantic poetry; memorized poems found in a romantic book of poems in my bookcase. Dramatically standing with one hand over his heart and the other out to the side in grand fashion stood Hipolito, the poet, reciting his favorites. The CW family theater happened often and included singing and silly magic acts. There is nothing like a house full of teens to keep things lively and hectic, but so much fun. As the kids grew, many of them believed they were old enough to take their independence, and some did. These are the 10 core kids we now lived with, worked together with and flooded CW with love. We, the adults — Ruth, Me, Carmen, and Maestro Juan — joined them on these evenings when the tourists were gone and relaxed into this fabulous playful energy.

The Tourist Groups Came

Many tourist groups came and stayed at our B&B as few accommodations were available in Urubamba in 1991. We all learned how to be waiters, cooks, food choppers, linen washers and bed changers in a big hurry if another group was coming in a few hours. With no washing machines, only big buckets to wash sheets and lines to dry them in the hot sun and breeze, we initially all jumped in to get the beds made with fresh clean sheets for the next group. This was a challenge, but we managed. We soon found and hired two ladies to help wash.

The breakfast part of the B&B meant we needed muffins to go with the coffee, and I was the only one who knew how to make them. Getting the correct amount of soda or baking powder in this altitude was a trick we finally figured out. The kids hovered around me to learn how to make breakfast muffins they really liked, so we developed a fun system. The pots were boiling away with CW staff and kids, lunch and oatmeal breakfast too, while we busied ourselves preparing for the tourists — on-the-job training and often including tasting.

Carmen was the head honcho in the tiny kitchen. A Canadian friend donated her old Kenmore gas stove and I retrieved it from Vancouver, Canada, and hauled it to Urubamba. It was perfect for this Urubamba B&B kitchen and along with the two-burner kerosene stove on the deck we could put a lot of pots to cook at once and served us well. I, along with Ruth and a child or two, lined up on our five-foot long counter and took orders from Carmen. *Chop onions, peal the yucca, and blend the peanut aji and aji amarilla.* She heated the oil one inch deep in the big fry pans. When sizzling, the yucca dipped in flour and egg go in, pan after pan, until there is enough for the whole gang of 20. We ate well and hearty in our house, with rarely a leftover or a skinny kid among us. The spicy hot peanut sauce went over the fried yucca — way too good for anyone watching their calories. Lucky for me you burn a lot of calories in CW and at 11,000 feet of Urubamba, just by walking around. Obesity is not seen in this village. Back to the chopping and peeling and blending we always had the most fun in the kitchen and pulling together managed to create big meals for 24 guests with enough extra for our gang. This took all-hands-on-deck with enough good jokes and stories and sharp knives to accomplish. And we did it all well. Still laughing and cleaning up our plates, one of the bigger boys cleaned up the bottom of the pot smacking his lips in the process. We sat on the floor or on low eight-inch stools or stood after the tourists had eaten and gone to their rooms. We were exhausted but content and still chattering away while the dishwashing began. No dishwasher here, rather many dishwashers, dish dryers, and put-awayers we were. In no time the mess was cleaned up, put away and the tables set for the 24 breakfasts at 6:00 a.m. Still laughing at Ruth's antics with one of the kids, we all headed to our rooms for five hours of sleep before we started the blender again making juice and frying eggs, making coffee. Breakfast at 6:00 a.m. We all jumped in voluntarily when a group arrived. No one had to ask for help as it was freely given, plus all the fun was in the kitchen, not to mention something good to eat. CW kids LOVE to eat.

The kids had the activities and work of any school child and the B&B activities and evening fun came second. Our kids were doing well in school and enjoyed their classes.

With our rooms to rent, Carmen's culinary skills, and the tourists being led to us, we made enough to feed, clothe, school and educate the gang, pay taxes, etc. For eight years this managed to provide a roof, food and all the basics needs for 15 abandoned street kids. We did great work in those early years on almost nothing but a wing and a prayer — many prayers.

School #712 and Princess Rosa

It was 1993. In addition to class assignments and other school activities, the public school #712 loved their festive events. The students voted to elect this year's school Princess and our Rosita won. Everyone was animated at home and participated in preparing for the parade with Princess Rosa sitting on top of the cab of our yellow truck in the lead. Maestro Juan (our all-round handyman and grounds man) and the boys: Chato, Efrain, Hipolito, Neto, Rato, Pepe, Marco and Roberto with help from our three girls: Santu, Naida and Rosa, gathered all the colorful sheets we had and that was two. Juan and the boys found long palms somewhere to cover and decorate the yellow truck for Rosa's place of honor in the parade. We were in the lead, thank goodness, because looking back now, I had become way too relaxed living in our mellow village and should have been horrified at my role in the special day parade as it applied to driving the truck.

Yellow and pink sheets covered a small table over the double cab and draped down the windshield to cover some of the hood and side windows. On the table we placed a wooden chair and put the very long palms on either side of the chair forming an arch over the chair where Rosa was perched all dressed in pink and a timid smile (inside she was bursting with excitement.) Two boys were under the table holding it from sliding off the roof of the truck.

To be able to drive and see too, I had a pyramid-shaped opening between the crisscross of the two sheets where they overlapped, the size of an open small book. Hunched over behind the wheel to peek out through this small pyramid opening, I drove the truck around the plaza in the parade. Several of our other kids and Ruth walked on each side of the truck to watch for little children too near the truck. My speed was very slow — no more than inches per hour.

The end result was everyone had a lot of fun except for me, too relieved to finally put the truck in the garage at the B&B and be rid of the stress I felt.

These sorts of makeshift events are frequent in our village and require a lot of creativity to make festive and fun with whatever was available, and very little was. So we joined in too and it was festive and fun.

The Scenic Road from Cusco to Urubamba

Returning from a two-week-long trip to California to visit my family and get supplies for CW, it was now necessary for me to shift gears and slow down. The beauty I saw looking out the van window was drawing me back to sweet Urubamba peace.

Maneuvering up Avenida Sol (the main street to the Cusco Plaza), a two-block line in front of Banco de Credito says it must be payday. 'Intel Peru' telephone company had a similar line of local residents waiting to pay their bills until the last day, or tomorrow their telephone lines would be dead. The Cathedral steps are sprinkled with women selling candles to residents stopping briefly to pray to the *'Black Christ'* (patron saint of Cusco) inside and located on the south side of the *'Plaza de Armas.'* Foot traffic strolls around children kicking a ball between them in the plaza, while tourists stop to admire their faces in the water fountain or just sit on a wooden bench to enjoy the beauty. The simple life of the Andes.

Winding through narrow cobblestone streets never meant for cars, we bump along, a little to the left — then right — and around to the San Pedro Market, the biggest in Cusco. Here we don't move at all. The street has been transformed into a giant sidewalk so thick with foot traffic my view is blue sky over bundled bodies in full skirts with brown arms hanging out of blue folds clutching ragged children and bumping into each other's babies strapped to their mothers' backs in hand-woven, colorful blankets. Behind the throngs somewhere are carts filled with tomatoes and avocados, sun-dried raisins, eggs and barrels of local black olives. This is where the local action is; the latest news, drama, socializing, theft, takes place and the home of sticky fingers.

Inch by inch, we move past the mob of hot, sweating, bodies. To the right are carts of bread of all shapes and sizes and another cart selling rolls of blue and black plastic sheets. The tires turn slowly, barely missing toes in tire sandals, and rows of plastic sheets on the asphalt piled with potatoes, big white and fat, brown round and tiny, long and yellow, red and smooth... all potatoes. One more right, and we are up and out of the market climbing over the hill and on our one-hour scenic drive to the Sacred Valley of the Incas.

Viewing the entire city from the hilltop before crossing to the other side and beginning the slow dip down through winding villages, tiny pueblos of Poroy and Chincheros, it is unbelievable how much Cusco has grown. The fields look like a huge patchwork quilt with their cultivated potatoes, corn, quinoa and cabbage. Truly, there is magic here; the beauty of sun-drenched cultivated fields up against peaks of huge snow-capped mountains and puffy white clouds pasted on true blue sky is breathtaking and never looks the same.

The van begins to wind down the switchback road to the floor of the valley and our home Urubamba. The old orange metal bridge takes us over the Urubamba river (Vilcanota) to the *Welcome to Urubamba* metal greeting now bent and bruised. Village life is like Potter Valley, California is to San Francisco, Andean style. Slow motion is the only motion here. The day begins and ends with the sun. Farmers live, cultivate and eat by seasons and rain. The easy, slow rhythm of man and nature is immediately noticed and a transitional experience for us high-speed Californians. At 11,000 feet, this valley is lower than Cusco's 13,000 feet, making breathing easier, but still an insult to my sea-level-adjusted body.

My heart soaks up the peace and my eyes the beauty; the tranquility my mind won't accept yet. It will take a few days to get my stuck foot off the racing throttle of my mind, but it will come.

The van turns right onto 'Calle Berriozabal' and stops in front of the pink painted adobe wall lining most of the street. The B&B name 'Urpi Wasi' (House of Peace) is written over an arch of river rock framing the entrance door and under a pagoda-style adobe red tile roof.

We have arrived. Inside, my eyes feast on white daisies, pink, lavender, blue and white wild flowers; to the right a shrine to Mother Mary surrounded many red, white and pink roses. *'Pacha Mama'* is sacred, respected and revered by the Quechua people and this sanctuary is a space held for us, to rest against her bosom.

My bag is delivered to my room by smiles with legs — the boxes for CW put somewhere to open later. It's time to nap; obligatory for the next two hours or the altitude will get me.

Urubamba Fundraising Years

The *Urpi Wasi B&B* in Urubamba changed our lives and our ability to financially continue CW, and in the process we all learned a lot. We blasted out to everyone on our mailing list, Facebook and a website that the founder had been leading tours to the Andes Inca wonderland and Machu Picchu to raise funds for CW Shelter and some responded.

My vision to buy this big old house with many bedrooms was to create a California-style B&B with a separate section big enough for all of us — and it paid off. This allowed me to stay in Peru longer and not travel to California every few months to fundraise, so I could organize and help fix up the B&B.

Urubamba Antics

Of course, there was always mischief with all these pre-teens and teens. When we moved into an old family home in the City of Urubamba in the Sacred Valley, it was to be a fundraising endeavor and better residence during the violent years for our core kids. It turned out to be much more. The core children learned many skills and some now worked in the restaurant and other service businesses as adults.

The POOL

Neglected and run down, the property covered about two acres. To the delight of the kids, it had an old swimming pool, still intact — but no filter, no heater and the only way to fill it was with the garden hose. Cleaning the monster water hole was the most fun. It seems it was built like a giant bathtub with one plug to let all the water out. So, every month we would pull the plug, drain it and all of us get inside with brushes on sticks or by hand and scrub the algae away and soon be squirting each other gleefully with the hose, then scrubbing some more, squirting some more to generally see that everyone had a good time. Putting kids together with water, sticks and general teenage antics meant we didn't get much pool cleaning done. On one occasion, the pool-cleaning project was hijacked by the kids acting out Shogun, a TV show I vaguely recalled about Japan years before. In the middle of scrubbing the big empty tub, abandoned brushes and sticks and brooms were lying all over the bottom, and the boys began acting out 'Shogun.' They jumped into the pool grabbing the brooms and sticks and began sword fighting with each other, and Ruth and Maestro Juan pretending to shout words in Japanese. Maestro then said seriously, *"I don't know Japanese,"* and Efrain responded, *"Just say anything in Quechua – who will know?"* and the game was on. The sticks became swords and they held sword fights all around the outside of the pool. Maestro Juan and Ruth were participating too, so I grabbed the video camera — this was too good to miss. We once sat through six hours of video over popcorn and Sangria at a CW family gathering years later. We laughed so hard we all had stomachaches from all the fun and popcorn — CW antics. The pool was the best fun. Even swimming in the melted ice water was okay on a sunny, warm day.

Suffice to say, it took almost a week to get the pool cleaned and filled again. I bought a special plastic cover in the States to try to heat up the frigid snow water with the sun. But it was too cold for all but the hardiest travelers and our kids. Locals mostly do not have hot water and would tell me how *'cold water helps the nerves.'* Andean cold water from the 'Chicon' Glacier we could see from our terrace was a really cold shower (so cold your head ached for an hour). Locals were less concerned since they didn't know how to swim, but they had a cautious curiosity. I did worry constantly that someone, a non-swimmer, would fall in — an adult or a child.

CW Skateboards

One day I looked out the window onto the street to see four of our boys running around and trying to ride what looked like skateboards. Where did they come from? I wondered, since we didn't have any. Being as creative as they were, I guessed they used their ingenuity and made them from what they saw on TV. When I came downstairs later and passed their dorm room, I noticed all the mattresses were on the floor. A closer look told me that all the wood slats needed to hold up the mattresses were missing. My high spirits vanished when it sunk in — not a happy moment. Seems they collected a bunch of Leche Gloria cans (canned milk cans) and nailed them to the wood slats. Of course, they were not wheels, but they could pretend. Well now they could pretend they had a bed to sleep on too since all the bunk beds were now on the floor. They had some explaining to do.

Death Comes Again

"Rae, can you come to Cusco? My father is dead." A hysterical Carmen blubbers into the telephone receiver.

"It will take me an hour to get there — wait for me," I tell her.

Accompanied by two of our boys well acquainted with death, I drive our truck over the mountain to Cusco from Urubamba, prepared for what is to come.

He lay on his cot just as the nun's found him in this senior home, untouched. Helping Carmen chang his clothes and wrap him in the blanket we brought, we left to buy the family wood coffin. Loaded in

125

the back of our truck it stuck out too far in our short-bed truck. The boys had to sit on the side next to the cab to be sure it stayed there. We all carried the coffin to his bedside and gently laid her father inside. It's raining now as we load the full coffin into the back of the truck and tie it down with rope the nuns gave us. Horrible thoughts race through my head of the big road holes in the long ride home to Urubamba — visions of a coffin and dad spilling out on the road sent a shudder through me. Covered with plastic and my jacket the boys assumed the position on top of the cab end of the coffin without a word for the wet hour-long journey home.

For two days our conference room was transformed into a place of mourning. The coffin lay in the center, and along both sides are big bulky and tall black candleholders and tall candles. Chairs line the walls filled with grieving family and friends. This time our space provides a warm and friendly environment for the all-night vigil. All night the candles burn; the prayers and low whispers fill the air. The kitchen light burns, sounds of chopping, and smells of something good simmering on the stove to feed the guardians of the spirit of the dead.

The priest said mass at 9:00 a.m., and by 10:00 the truck was loaded with the coffin, and all the relatives who could enter did. I drove this sad party to the cemetery with shovels for all who were strong enough to help dig the grave.

The men took turns digging ceremoniously and silently. Carmen and the others removed a shovelful first, and in 40 minutes the hole was dug, and he was lowered inside. A circle formed around the grave and flowers were cast along with prayers for a safe journey. One by one, each took their turn returning shovelful after shovelful until the coffin was covered in a blanket of earth. Silence again. Slowly, a few went to get the nearby chicha (Andean corn beer). Filling the small water glass — first a splash on mother earth — and then one by one each swallows a glassful until all had a turn, sending prayers up with the drink.

CHAPTER 13

CW Adult Life in 'Urpi Wasi B&B'

*"Women are realists, the glue that holds society together.
They bring a reverence to life that's instinctual, not just
intellectual."* — Teresa Heinz Kerry

1996 — CW Red Truck Blowout

I WAS WARNED not to make the trip over the mountain from Cusco
and back to Urubamba after dark alone, but I am used to driving on
quiet country roads in rural California, so paid little attention to the
local advice. Our supplies were needed in Urubamba today, and so
many times I had made this run alone in our tired old yellow truck
with no problems. What problem could I possibly have in this brand
new shiny red 4x4 Toyota truck, a donation from Toyota Lima?

Rushing around Cusco filling the double cab with toilet paper,
oil, sacks of flour and sugar and boxes of miscellaneous food items in
Cusco and securing two tanks of propane tied to the grate up against
the window in the bed of the truck, and I was on my way. It was not
quite dark, and the asphalt road was good on the many turns climbing and also descending the switchback road into the sacred valley where we now lived. A very productive trip: notary papers were

127

signed, supplies purchased and loaded, and a quick lunch with my friend and café owner Marta — my spirits were up. I put a cassette in the player and sang along with my favorite chant 'Om Tare.'

Then it happened. A very loud double BANG BANG interrupted my song as my two left tires blew out simultaneously, throwing the loaded truck out of control and sliding sideways, threatening to roll or slide off the road and down the precipice on the opposite side of the road. I remember thinking: *I guess my work is done here,* and just then the truck landed, plop, on its four wheels, and stopped on the edge. In a crazy moment of humor, I said, *I guess not!* Then I looked out my door window down into the deep ravine and realized how close to going down there I was still. I climbed out the other side of the cab and stood there looking at my situation. Alone on this curve, I recalled the local warnings that no one will stop their car on these desolate roads at night — never, ever. Many terrorist traps have been set this way.

Standing on the lonely road, I was just beginning to worry when an old beat-up truck came around the corner; one headlight was out. The driver slowed and looked me over, then stopped. His wife stayed in the car. He told me in gentle Spanish, *"Don't worry mama. I won't leave you alone."* He offered to try to pull out my new four-wheel drive with his old truck. It was clear his truck couldn't handle the job and he couldn't survive the loss. When I said I didn't want to hurt his truck, he offered to try to drive mine, hanging precariously off the road and ready to slide down the hill. He came to have a closer look. My two left tires were in shreds and the truck sat on the rims. I knew I had only one spare. He offered to drive it out for me, but that generous offer alarmed me looking at his patched-up, old truck. He had never driven a 4X4 truck, and I feared he might go down into the ravine with the truck.

Courage rose in me. I thanked him and told him I really needed him to help me be brave and guide me out. He agreed. I climbed into the cab the way I got out and started the engine. I engaged the 4-wheel drive and it popped right out onto the pavement, even though the back left rim was not in contact with the ground. I loved this new 4X4 truck, the tires were ruined, there was only one spare, but I was a happy woman. No one was hurt, and the propane tanks were intact, and with this little farmer standing at my side, my trembling subsided a little.

I reached for the tire lug nut key in my ashtray to find it was gone, creating a big problem to change a tire. This was a bad time in Peru around terrorism and a foreign woman alone was always a bad idea — driving alone worse. My family and friends in California were always worried for me, yet I never felt any threat or fear. Suddenly another car pulled up, and another, and another.

While I stood considering my options, a bus came by from Urubamba and stopped to see if I needed help. I gave them the name of the Goodyear tire dealer I knew in Cusco and a note to give him asking that he please bring me a tire. The entire busload was interested in my dilemma and wanted to be helpful. I thanked them all and off they went to Cusco with my note. Shortly after that a car came by heading to Urubamba and I sent a note to Ruth and our house that I was OK but waiting for tires from Cusco.

From around the corner a taxi appeared from Cusco with Ruth's mother telling the driver to stop and waving at me. A thermos of hot coffee and cups were handed to me while I convinced her I was fine, and tires were on their way. I thanked her and she left to return back to her Cusco restaurant.

The familiar yellow truck of our neighbor in Urubamba came loaded with CW kids and Ruth, another thermos of coffee and ready to help. I sent them back too, since the tires were coming.

By then it was pitch black and I was standing alone on the side of the road when a big rig, with headlights so bright it looked like a jet liner on the pavement, pulled up. I asked them if they would help me with tools to remove the lug nuts, since my security lock key had been stolen. The other cars had no tools to do the job. They informed me they had heard I was in trouble and had come from the Cachymayu Fertilizer plant down in the ravine to help me and would take the car and me to the plant for safety.

By then I was choked up with emotion at the many hands reaching out to help me. This troubled country with all of the corruption and injustices that are considered normal here evaporated for me then. Here was more help in troubled times for a stranger than I could ever hope for in my own country. The shredded tires seemed unimportant to me. Something else was happening.

I thanked them also and told them tires were on the way, but I did need help getting the tires off with no lug nut key. Several men jumped down and began to work on the lug nut locks with their tools and soon their fingers were dripping blood. I was so moved by the help I was being given by just about everyone that passed, it was overwhelming. To think that my family worried about me in the land of unrest and unknown scary things made me smile. I am hardly alone ever. It seems that I stand out more than I realized — everyone knew who I was and where I lived and offered help.

Suddenly in the dark I saw the Goodyear truck with tires piled up to the top of the cab. The driver was with his wife and son in the cab and looked less than happy. He leaned out the window and told me I neglected to send the size of the tire I needed, so he brought them all. That didn't feel so good. Sadly, I probably interrupted his dinner to load and bring me so many tires. This was my life in Urubamba, Peru.

Returning to The Sacred Valley from California

The death of my father called me back to California, and I was gone a month. Returning home to Urubamba felt wonderful. Our simple, loving and cooperative lifestyle I had learned to value.

The heavy door opened letting in fresh crisp Cusco air and sunlight into the cabin. In no rush, I planned to wait until the plane was empty. Then it is down the metal stairs, always juggling a heavy bag in each hand until they hurt. Already my chest is getting tight and I feel air hunger. I wonder how much longer I can do this — a lot longer. Stepping onto the asphalt, I am grateful this is the end of the line. My wheeled carry-on seems to know where to go, and we are off to the conveyor belt of luggage.

Passengers surround the conveyer belt in the baggage claim area and are in a hurry when I get there. Today I am one of the smiling returning just watching and in no hurry. No bags appear yet, so I scan the doors for CW family faces. There they are: Ruth, the kids, and Juan — waving madly, lighting up my day. Another grim-faced door security man is watching them too and won't let them inside. Ruth and I start our routine (we are pros at his by now), and I begin to work on the guard using my well-rehearsed pained look, *"Senor, por favor, necesito ayuda de mis amigos... no puedo sola,"* disgusting groveling for a feminist woman. He doesn't let them through, so while I jabber away and further confuse the issue, he turns away bored with this line he has heard before. Sometimes this works, but this time it didn't. But Ruth and Efrain slipped through the pushing and shoving crowd of taxi hustlers, hotel sign-carrying peddlers and independent tour guide gropers. Hipolito and Juan couldn't get through. They smiled just the same. Warm generous hugs are exchanged, while one eye guards my loaded cart of bags. Everyone talks at once and we burst out laughing. Efrain spots the suitcases and boxes on the conveyer belt and in minutes we have them all distributed among us. Filing out and through the crowd in my gringa body is a test of my ability to fend off the overly competitive hustlers in all sizes and shapes wanting some green.

Coming home to Urubamba now feels sad and changed. CW is moving forward and planning to return to Cusco once there is a final sale on 'Urpi Wasi.' I am here to speak to a potential buyer about just that. Living in Urubamba has been very special, not only for me but for the kids too. They made friends, got an education and finished high school and learned many practical skills. Some moved on to begin their adult lives and others enrolled at the University. Ruth and I are in the process of reorganizing CW completely to educate forgotten little girls so that they never are so desperate that they want to abandon their children.

Experts that we are, in minutes we are loaded into a mini-van and on our way into town. Once away from the swarm, I allow myself to relax and breathe deeply and slowly, letting every O2 molecule have time to hook up. Still, I feel light-headed and fuzzy-brained, an early warning of 'Soroche' (altitude sickness). If I don't lie down and nap soon, I will be miserable, involuntarily.

Always touching to come home when I first see the busy area around the city. Three-wheeled carts carrying boxes and corn file by on a side street where the Ttio morning market is bustling. A statue of the Inca Pachacutq towers over the island ovalo and passing traffic, a reminder that this city was home to the Inca Empire. Foot traffic dominates here, the reverse of California, and sidewalks are heavily scattered with business people, vendors and shoppers.

Weaving our way through town and the big market, soon we are up and out of the market climbing up the hill and over for the one-hour drive to the Sacred Valley of the Incas and our home in Urubamba. Peru has been my home for 10 years, and I am feeling a somber shift in me.

The van begins the zig-zag down the mountain to the Sacred Valley and will enter the slow flow of the valley and our home 'Urubamba'. The old orange metal bridge still takes us over the Urubamba River (Vilcanota) to be welcomed by the 'Welcome to Urubamba' battered metal sign looking worse all the time — both are in need of repair or replacement.

Calle Berriozabal is my street and we stop in front of our B&B 'Urpi Wasi' (House of Peace) and the entrance door to my home. The Chicuchas Wasi family home feels wonderful. The first thing you see coming through the door is the statue of Mother Mary surrounded by her grotto; an egg-shaped cover of stones that cover her white statue, with candles and colorful flowers everywhere in the larger garden. We have been blessed to stumble onto this big family home that became a small sanctuary that we lived in during the difficult political years of Peru and were protected in this space protected by the Mother.

It is that time again, to lie down and sleep and let my body adjust to the altitude.

Urubamba Laundry Day & Roberto

In Urubamba the chores were the same as in the city of Cusco, but the space was much larger with so many more creative ways to escape this chore.

On the left side of our large country house situated on a two-acre cultivated compound with fruit trees, potatoes and other vegetables, were two large cement sinks, side by side, where all of our washing would take place. The ice-cold water melted from the glacier up the mountain on our left and came through our water spigot along with an occasional frog or other bugs. We also still had our big red plastic wash buckets for more washing when we had all the tourist sheets to wash from 23 beds in the B&B.

The day was sunny, warm and had a big cloudless blue sky and perfect to do our personal wash. Our nine resident kids gathered their dirty clothes and the radio, and we gathered out around this mostly grassy area to get to work. Like any washday with that many teens and a little Latin music, the fun was about to begin. Soapsuds were splashed on the heads of those trying to wash (the three girls), but the playful boys (there were six) delighted in tormenting the girls. By the time the girls had their laundry washed and up on the line, they got even with the boys, and in minutes no one was dry or even cared that the water was so cold. Laughter won out and the music kept the boys dancing in the cement sinks on their clothes to wash them. We adults always had to check their rooms to see that ALL the clothes were actually washed, and today it seemed that they were.

After so much effort washing, everyone had worked up an appetite and headed to our little downstairs private old adobe kitchen and rammed-earth stove (Fogon). Food never tastes as good on a modern gas stove. Bellies full, everyone headed to rest or read or basically take a nap.

Later in the day, Maestro Juan came to talk to me. *"Mamma, I want to show you something,"* and I followed him into the garden and yard. The property was divided with river rock walks and by many Cypress trees, and they created walls around the larger garden rooms. Pointing up into a tall Cypress 12-15 feet tall was a white bundle. He has his ladder out and pulled it down for a look. It appeared to be a sheet that was tied up in the Cypress tree to hide the dirty clothes inside — Roberto's clothes. He was the teenage boy most allergic to chores of any kind. One look at the quantity of dirty clothes he now must wash, I wondered what he actually had to wear. Summer weather was warm, so you could run around in shorts for a few months, but then you would need warmer clothes. Roberto spent the next few days washing his clothes, his sheets and his towels. In washing that much, I am guessing he covered the shower requirement since the other kids were around to hose him down and to heckle him for getting caught.

CHAPTER 14

Chicuchas Wasi Moves On

"Without learning, we are in the dark."
— Numada, 14-year-old Somali student

BY 1996, MANY of our resident children were young adults and had moved on. Three of our more serious students — Efrain 17 and Hipolito 16 were preparing for University after high school graduation; Rosa 14 received a full-ride scholarship to Ursuline High School in California. The other shelter children were out creating their adult life with the tools they learned in CW. Several were opening a business, a bar, auto repair or drive taxis, etc.

Notably, Efrain and Hipolito (from the early CW Shelter), were deep in study, but still found a minute here and there to lend a helping hand to these little ones in sweet and caring ways. Efrain has been offered a scholarship at a local College to prepare him for a career in tourism, quite an achievement for a boy with his background. Efrain has a big heart and has a habit of bringing young children home in need of a meal, clothes and shoes that CW has ready for these emergencies. Rosa is on a high school scholarship in California and will graduate in May 1999 from Ursuline High School and will enter Sonoma State University. Our three shining stars have made us proud, and this is just the beginning. Ruth, using her persuasive talents, convinced the best University in Cusco to accept Hipolito, the third in his high school class. At every encounter, the high school principal praises our boys, their enthusiasm, hard work and strong desire to achieve academically. Our boys fully understand the necessity of education if they are to be of any help to themselves and their families. They will continue in CW to help Ruth and as their home base to complete their University education. The extended family of CW is growing.

Our work with hundreds of abandoned street children changed their lives and futures forever and impacted many more children who entered CW over the years, through our door either to live in residence or to participate in the CW vocational school to learn to market their folk art. During the 10 years of our CW Shelter, we created an atmosphere of love that surrounded everyone in the house, especially the children were filled with this energy. Stories were shared and laughter welcomed while learning serious living skills they would need as adults when the time came and they as young adults felt ready to begin their independent lives. During those 10 years working and learning the reality of the abandoned child, we learned through stories the street kids shared, the reality of their families. CW recognized the need to make a bigger impact.

A year later CW was reorganizing to focus on education for the poor indigenous girls of rural Cusco and would return to the Cusco house to continue this plan. It was decided that I should return to California and reorganize how we fund this new plan and hunt for new creative ideas.

Urubamba was changing, and foreigners were moving in to take advantage of the booming tourist industry in the Sacred Valley. Big expensive hotels began to appear, and it was clear that we had done well with our basic B&B, but to stay and compete with the money that this business would now need was not our focus or mission. In addition, the only English speaker was returning to California.

Urpi Wasi no longer served our mission, and the B&B was sold to local ceramic artists to grow their production for international exportation. All of the resident kids by then had graduated from high school and gone off to work. Efrain and Hipolito went to the Cusco University and were living in the Cusco house. Rosa was in California attending Sonoma State University in the Nursing program. The CW kids learned a lot over the 8-9 years we lived in and operated the B&B. They learned to cook special and practical dishes, bake cakes and muffins and cookies, they learned to be waiters, speak a bit of English, Italian and more. Chicuchas Wasi was turning the page; our next chapter was beginning to happen.

And after 10 years hands-on, I returned in 1997 to California to do CW Administrative and Fundraising work.

Urubamba
Chicuchas Wasi School Experiment

Almond preschool eyes, glazed over, dull
Dark holes in a somber tiny face
Here, in Ruth's presence.
Here, 5 hours a day.
Here, the light flips on.
Coffee brown marbles become
Shiny pools of liquid energy.
Unbound potential — Unbound hope — Unbound opportunity.
Female burden is charged with possibility.

Ruth and I developed a plan to educate poor girls in 1996, while still in Urubamba. That same year, Ruth opened an experimental class for four-year-old little girls in our separate section away from the B&B in our private area of the buildings to see if we could persuade their mothers to allow them to go to school. CW experimental class served only a handful of girls that year; it was difficult for parents to under-stand the value of allowing their daughters to go to school. It was with great effort that Ruth Uribe, our School Director, managed to persuade parents that it was worth the effort to educate a girl, when the families so strongly believed she would be more valuable helping domestically at home. In those first CW School classes, we could see the changes in our students almost immediately, eagerness replaced disinterest.

When I arrived in July, the CW experimental classroom was bubbling with enthusiasm. A buzz of giggles and whispers, scampering feet, and sliding desks filled the hall and classroom. Little brown bodies and big twinkling black eyes were covered with blue, red, and yellow colored animals printed on black smocks with canary yellow sleeves, pushing their way through the door, each wanting to be first. Joining tiny hands, they formed a circle in the middle of a round of desks. Ruth entered the center and turned slowly to look at each pair of eyes smiling back at her. You could have heard a pin drop. Every girl returned her silent greeting and then a loud *"Buenas Dias, Profesora"* leaped from those smiles in unison. Gloria, our student teacher, entered the circle leading all in a prayer song of gratitude to Mother Mary.

The mood became calm, respectful, and orderly, and each child took her seat placing pencils, colors, and paper on top of her desk, ready for the lessons. The first lesson was on hygiene. Gloria asked four-year-old Monica if she remembered to brush her teeth this morning. A toothbrush shot up in the air, held proudly in her tight fist, eyes eager, smiling. Milagros held up hers too, shyly, eyes down, from across the room. One by one toothbrushes popped up around the circle.

Next came Peruvian geography. Against the wall was a giant map of Peru and each child was asked to draw with their colors on their paper, their Peru. Rosita went to the map and pointed to Cusco. Then came questions and talk of their participation in Peru's Independence Day parade, *Fiestas Patrias.* All schools in Peru participate in the parade of Peru's Independence. Each child carefully wrote her name and age on her drawing, and then it was snack time — juice and bread for all.

By 11:30, there was so much racket outside in the street

(boom-boom-boom-dada- boom-boom-boom-dada) as every school child in Urubamba filled every available street to practice marching for the parade. The repetitive beat of the marching music filled the space in, around, and through our classroom and presented a good time for recreation *recreo* and marching practice for our class on the blacktop. Ruth in the lead and Gloria in the rear assisted the littlest straggler button up her new smock after a bathroom run.

Happy little Chicuchas girls marched in circles, back and forth, in and out, some wandering off here and some there. We needed a bit more practice, but our adorable four-year-olds representing their brand-new school showed off their tiny slice of life in Urubamba.

I wish to thank each and every one of you who have held our hand for the many years of our existence. Chicuchas Wasi is small, but mighty, and we are making a difference. Because of you, these children will reach far.

With all the changes whirling around us and Rae returning to California, our B&B *Urpi Wasi* had lost its rudder and English speaker to manage the tourists at a time that new modern hotels were popping up all over. The boys were now studying in Cusco and everyone was moving on; it was time to let *Urpi Wasi* (House of Peace) return into local hands and it was sold. But the wonderful memories we will keep.

Child abandonment by desperate, uneducated mothers unable to provide for their children will not end without educating daughters. With 10 years' experience working and learning the reality of the abandoned street children, Ruth and I recognized we needed to make a bigger impact. We reorganized Chicuchas Wasi as a School for the Poor Underserved Girl, free of charge to their families. In the rural parts of Cusco, poor indigenous girls do not attend school and often will be the most likely to abandon their child if abandoned by their male provider.

Ruth had recruited Gloria earlier (a student teacher) to join the team and together they moved and grew the school returning to Cusco.

It was clear my presence will be needed as CW fundraiser back in California, leaving Ruth to the difficult process of convincing mothers to send their daughters to school. Ruth wanted to open the formal school in Cusco, so CW returned to Cusco — entirely administered and operated by local Cusco educators — and ever since we have had great success meeting the needs of this rural community and changing the lives of their daughters, no longer destined to a life of poverty.

When I returned to California in 1997, I needed to learn new skills to take on the serious fundraising the new school would require as it grew. This new responsibility would require expanding my computer skills, with web design, social media use, online fundraising and learning to do modern day grant writing. I enrolled at my local junior college to learn how to do all the things I needed to do on the computer to promote a nonprofit. It worked. It really did work.

Maybe too much, as I am now glued to my desktop most days, my new almost full-time job, for the love of our CW girls of course. CW has benefited from the new ability to attract new supporters and friends with newsletters and our Facebook reach.

In Peru, Efrain is a well-known tour guide today who tells his story of growing up in Chicuchas Wasi and now taking all his groups to visit CW and the students first-hand. Many of these new friends have become supporters, and their donations allow us to take more students at no cost to families. This has been a slow process, and CW is still growing.

CHAPTER **15**

Rae's Last Visit to 'Urpi Wasi'

"Dream as if you will live forever. Live as if you will die today." — James Dean

A Typical Week

I AWAKE AT 8:00 a.m., groggy but rested. All six alpaca blankets are in the same position they were in when I entered the bed at 9:00 p.m. last night, unmoved as if covering a stiff cadaver all night. Yesterday I arrived with my head full of altitude cotton and a body rebelling at the 24 hours of sardine-like travel and burro-like treatment. It only wanted one thing — to be horizontal, to sleep. Yet, when my eyes landed on Ruth, then Efrain and Erik at the airport gate, it was like a visceral shot of something I can't put my finger on, lifting, filling, energizing, hugging and a warm fuzzy; like a beautiful blooming rose garden in the middle of a Tahoe winter. Something in me just let go and surrendered to this love. On the hour drive to Urubamba, mouth kicked in and the Spanish synapses were on a roll. I dove deep into the black eyes facing me while her rapid-fire Spanish washed over me. In my peripheral vision I saw the smiling, hugging eyes of welcome from Erik, her new husband, and the serious/playful face of Efrain. No one had a chance, they had to wait until Ruth and I had exhausted ourselves and then it would be their turn. I don't even remember if the jagged peaks were topped with snow, of if the fields were just harvested or just blooming. It was then I remembered the tortellini and the pesto sauce in my daypack. Ruth squealed with delight and hugged them to her, warming the defrosted meal I worried could spoil during the trip. I said nothing; just watched her eyes float around in her head while hugging harder. She was thanking me and telling me how much she missed me and would settle to hug the tortellini for now.

Two big suitcases and my daypack were delivered with me to my now temporary home. The upstairs pink painted room in the new building is to be mine for the next two weeks. *Bienvenida a Casa de Todo tu Familia de CW* was plastered on the wall in a poster covered with red painted roses with green stems and a dingle leaf. A white porcelain bud vase sat on the little table filled with someone's personal stuff and was filled with red and white roses. Plaid blue and pink flannel sheets peaked out from under the yellow spread. Two soft pillows with matching cases were at the head so I could read at night. A bedside table and lamp waited quietly for the long night we would share. The air was filled with love and anticipation. There is no inside heating in Urubamba and it was dead winter, but the room was warm. "Rae, a la mesa" Hipolito yells from the bottom of my stairs. I notice I am hungry, and he prepared my favorite Quinoa soup for a late lunch. All nine of us filed into the dining room where nine bowls of steaming soup filled each green place mat on the round table. Fernando appeared with the old black and white TV dangling off his arm, plugged it in and attached the broken antenna, more or less, so the final quarter of the Championship soccer game between Brazil and France would not be missed. The entire house is mesmerized by a team of tan men in green shorts trying to get a black and white ball into their goal basket and away from the team of white men in white shorts.

GOAL, GOAL, GOAL!!! shouts come from the TV. Fists pound on the table almost spilling Hipolito's culinary efforts. France and the green shorts won the Championship. A momentary glumness mingles with the slurping sounds of the hot liquid.

Bellies full, everyone heads out to lay in the grass or to their rooms. I have the urge to write but looking at my notepad and small zipper bag of pens, I lose my inspiration. Listen to me. I am spoiled rotten; I want my computer back in California. When I asked Ruth if she needed our little MAC computer for the next few hours, she said no and handed it to me. Great! It is plugged in and ready to go, transformer and surge protector in place. This little workhorse always seems to work. In 15 years, it has crashed only once that I know of.

La Casa de Los Espiritos aired on 5, one of our two TV channels, last night. Huddled around it, and a huge bowl of fresh-popped popcorn sprinkled with grated cheese and a pitcher of sangria with tiny chopped apples and bananas floating on top and spiked with sprite to stretch the wine, sat the entire residence of CW plus a teenage neighbor. We wrapped up in blankets and settled in to be devoured by the historic plot. The popcorn was gone before the first commercial; the sangria was soon to follow. Sleep was tugging at me and won out finally.

I was asleep in minutes only to waken at 1:00 a.m. wide-awake listening to our dog bark at the neighboring canine watchmen. At 2:00, I gave up the idea of sleep in favor of reading Laurel's Kitchen introduction written by Carol Flinders, an author I had just met before the trip at a reading on a new book. I doubt I finished a paragraph when I drifted too far and couldn't pull back. I slept.

Roosters begin the day here at 4:30 a.m., and so do I. I dragged myself from the warm, heavy blankets to empty a threatening bladder in my little white porcelain-coated basin. The sound of urine hitting the metal (tinkleeeee, tinkleeee, tinkleeeee) in the silence woke me up. It was then my toes landed in something wet and I realized I had missed. A bit of a scramble with only tissue to mop it up, and I was fast asleep again.

Ding-dong. Nobody was moving. Ding-dong, ding-ding-ding-dooooooong! — and I heard voices and doors closing. Ruth is tapping on my door. *"Rae, there is someone here to see you about the B&B for sale."*

I can't believe this, my swollen head complained, on my third and worse day at 10,000 feet. I stumbled out of bed, trying not to step on the wet spot, threw on my sweats, and navigated my way down the stairs carefully to the bathroom. Ice-cold water straight from Chicon is usually enough to do it, but my head didn't respond. My frozen teeth after brushing only felt frozen. The cotton between my ears was hard to get rid of.

I ran to the dining room where a young man in casual tired street clothes stood and introduced himself as Alejandro, representing his uncle in Lima. I gave him the information he wanted about the sale of the property, exchanged names and phone numbers, and he left. I downed coffee and a fist full of vitamins and returned to finish dressing for the day.

Ruth and I sat on her bed upstairs in her bedroom talking about the past ups and the horrible downs we have had. We laughed, and a few tears fell. And we talked about the future and all we have learned together. Just then, her husband came home. It was 11:30 AM, July 13, 1998.

Ruth was still in her bathrobe, and we were deep in conversation; he was surprised. Laughing together a minute, I left them to go to my room.

"Rae, a la mesa" rings out in the patio — Hipolito is the proud cook again. Fried yucca with aji de mani is my favorite. I ate and burned, ate and burned; then put out the fire with ice-cold water. Now lying on my bed nursing a heavy and unhappy gut, I recalled I always do this. How old must I be to learn?

Tuesday, July 14, 1998

My head is still full of cotton until noon when my eyes fully open. The only good part is that all of my wrinkles have stretched out and I don't have to get up to pee during the night. Sleep here takes on a different definition. I sleep all night. I mean I really sleep — deep, deeper than any other time. Something intangible permeates the air with peace and harmony inside these walls, and at night the angels hold us in their arms.

The day was full of kitchen laughter, stories and cooking — then eating or thinking about eating; something the people here do a lot. By 6:30 PM, I was ready to get comfortable. Ruth, Gloria and I had planned a movie (video) — that is, if Gloria could find one and bring it from Cusco by the last bus. We made popcorn and a visiting Luis joined in and grated the cheese on top. We fought as we slid our hands under the white puffs hunting for large clumps of cheese to smash the puffs onto from the bottom.

We huddled around the tiny kitchen, oblivious to its size; Hipo and Fernando heating leftover soup and slurping it down, Nheomi quietly spooning down hot quinoa soup, and the rest of us laughingly jamming brown, yellow and white hands down into the huge bowl of white corn.

Gloria arrived with the full version of "The House of Spirits." Cups of hot herbal tea "mate" in hand, we followed Ruth hugging the big bowl to the TV room and sat mesmerized for the next two hours.

Wednesday, July 15, 1998

Shouts of "papas, cebolla, manzanas" woke me at 7:00, and I wondered where I was. The usual roosters went unnoticed in the drone of voices and movement of carts and trucks outside.

What is going on out there? I wondered, and got up, threw the borrowed robe over my long-johns and went to see. The entire Urubamba market was outside our house in the street. Hawkers, venders, and people — hundreds of people — were milling around carts and blankets of produce spread out on the ground. Indian women with full skirts and felt box hats from their village sat behind their potatoes, or carrots, or sacks of dried *choclo,* big hominy like corn on the ground.

By the time I got dressed and went to the front door to have a look and get a few pictures, Maestro Juan had managed to shoo them away from the front of our house with the help of a garden house. I looked at him shocked and said, *Con mangera (with the hose)?* Then I noticed it was the cut end of the hose, about three feet long, but it worked. He cleared the path to our door.

By the time I entered the kitchen for breakfast — a cup of watery but good Quaker sweet oatmeal — the grumbling had simmered down to a mumble. The Wednesday market has spread out to our street over the last two weeks while the new covered market area is being built. Ruth was wild.

"Last Wednesday, I couldn't even get out the front door without climbing over piles of garlic and onions and people," she huffed. A man and two women had a pushing-shouting fight in front of the door, while one of the women bent over and flipped up her skirt revealing round buttocks to the man receiving most of the shouts. She went on to elaborate on the indignity of it all and at our front door. *Grumph!*

I should have seen the omen; this would be a change from the peaceful, calm days since I arrived. Ruth was on the phone talking to some military official about Hipolito and Fernando. It seems they are ripe for the picking and the word is out; the army truck will be in town to do just that today. She is putting on the charm: *"Si pues, puedes ayudarnos, no Tio (uncle)?"* So, we have *Barra* (muscle) again, an uncle, thank god. He tells her to not let the boys out and he will come from Cusco to take care of the matter at 10:00. He didn't show, and the boys were confined to the house — no school today. The look of pain on their faces was almost believable.

Back to the phone and more of the *"Si Tio, por favor Tio, 2:00 en la tarde si, gracias tio."* Relieved, she handed me the Military registration cards for Hipolito and Fernando, the keys to her room, and headed to the paradero (bus stop) to catch the bus to Cusco. I am less than pleased with this plan. I will meet her uncle, some military hot shot, with the boys in tow and go to the coliseum and risk delivering them into the truck. Remembering a prior same-scenario, I don't handle it well when they try to get graft out of me. This does not go well with a gringa in the lead — not this gringa anyway. Ruth must have forgotten.

I sent Gloria to meet him and kept the boys in the house — once picked up, it is REALLY hard to get them out, unwilling to take the risk. She returns with him in the red Toyota 4x4 from the consejo, which gives me food for thought. This is the mayor's truck??? We head — Tio hot shot, Gloria, Hipolito, Fernando and me — to the coliseum. Teenage boys and girls in grey school uniforms hang together in 2's and 3's outside the closed door.

Worried peasant parents hover around, fear on their faces. Campesino fathers with reddened eyes stand without moving. The bus arrives to take the boys to the military base cartel in Cusco. I push our boys into the shadows of a garage. El Tio hot shot has gone inside to look for his patas (buddies), the brass hot-shots, and returned to say they have gone to lunch and will be back any minute.

At 3:30, they still haven't returned, so he goes to look for them, in a restaurant/bar. This is beginning to smell like trouble. Finally, he returns to say he couldn't find them. Meanwhile, the boys have come out of the shadows and are leaning against a light pole. I tell them they will look good in military green for two years, and they faded back to the shadows. Tio hot-shot says not to worry he will take care of everything and the boys won't even have to go inside the building. I remember trying to talk to beer-empowered brass in the past and cringe. *The temptation and problem with this picture is me, the gringa, walking dollar, North American millionaire, and the I-want-some syndrome.*

Gloria and I huddle for a minute and I tell her that with me here things could go bad, very bad. She agrees and asks me if I don't have a meeting where I have to be. I apologize to Tio hot-shot and evaporate before anyone else sees their potential fortune evaporate. At 4:00 PM, Gloria and the boys return home. It is all fixed, stamp-stamp-stamp. They are home free and can return to school tomorrow.

Relieved, we head to the kitchen to look for something, anything, to eat. This is the part of Peru I hate, I mean really dislike, abhor, and don't want to be a part of anymore. Our boys can finish high school, get out of military duty because of barra, while the lowest rung of the ladder, the cholos (pesants) from the campo (rural areas), fill the ranks.

CHAPTER **16**

CW Has Strong Bones

"Love is the bridge between you and everything."
— Rumi

Why I Chose Education

Ruth Uribe (CW School Creator, Administrator/Director)

"I FEEL LIKE I am a super fortunate person because the Mother has chosen me to be her instrument, with the privilege to live incredible experiences and to meet such wonderful people in my life. I know this is true and I feel very special. Someone once said to me when I decided to study education that I would just be one teacher more. It made me think that it is not what we chose to be or study, because there is a hidden objective that we cannot see from the outside, but that can grow big inside.

We make many decisions in life that suit us materially, that we do not really think about. What is our vocation? What makes us feel like a better woman, man, person? By giving ourselves fully to the Mother, she will make sure we get what we need.

I have had wonderful female role models: Divine Mother fills me with Love, my mom was the most wonderful woman; wise and loving.

Rae is my friend, mother, daughter and sister. She taught me to see the world with simplicity and today as an incredible woman who is not afraid of challenges, who is reinventing herself as they appear. She is a great model for me.

When I was in the last year of my college education for a career in Education, I met Rae. She came one day with the children to the Church hot meal program where I was a volunteer. Later she invited me to a workshop organized by Chicuchas Wasi and funded by UNICEF to bring together all the organizations that worked with street children in Cusco.

That is when I began volunteering at CW, at first on weekends. The children called me Aunt Ruth. Little by little, my commitment grew, and it soon was time to make the decision of my life. At that time, I was a teacher for the Ministry of Education and in a good teaching position that I won in a challenge. I had a good reliable salary and many future possibilities for promotion and my parents were very proud of my progress and position.

When the time came, and I communicated my decision to join CW, my mother did not understand, but she supported me. However, my father did not understand and reacted differently. He asked me: 'How can you leave a secure job with a future?' He thought his daughters would only leave home to be married or to become nuns and those were his words! He stopped talking to me for two years; this was difficult for me since I felt that this move was very special for me. To think that he did not see THIS and that I did not have his approval made me feel very bad. I had the support of my mother, an incredibly wise woman.

Soon I moved to CW in Urubamba with Rae and the children. We were doing something to really improve the immediate situation of the street children by creating the emergency Shelter project. The Shelter opened in '87 in the small Cusco house before relocating to Urubamba in '90. The children could sleep, have their meals, study in a home like shelter, but like any project not all volunteers come with the same objective of service and in Cusco that was a problem. Rae and I think alike. We wanted to become more effective and to help more children because in the Cusco Chicuchas Wasi home we had many children who needed more. So, I began to investigate the real situations of these abandoned children.

It was on one of those days that I went to the marginal zone of Cusco where street children congregated to do my study. I found a woman of incredible patience; tired and returning from her job pushing her kerosene tricycle. It was about 4:00 p.m. when I approached and asked her to answer some questions. She told me: 'No, Mamita, I do not have time, I have to cook.' So, I told her, 'I will help you,' and while I was peeling the lima beans, I was given her age of 40. Her marital status was cohabiting, but for her that was married, and she had five children. 'And your partner — where does he work?' 'He travels to the jungle looking for gold; sometimes is gone many months, sometimes he brings money and sometimes not.' I asked her if she supports the family. She told me, 'Well, yes!' At the time I noticed a man a little older with a young woman in the middle of their patio with a mud floor. I asked her if he was her husband. She said yes, I asked her if the girl was her daughter, and she said no. Then she gave me an answer that would change my vision of everything. She told me that this young woman was her husband's partner. I was stunned. She added very fast and angrily, 'Mamita, you do not know anything — here in my neighborhood if you do not have a man nobody respects you, nobody listens to you.' For her she didn't care. She needed the image of a man in her house. It was incredible. She maintained the entire family, worked hard, but did not feel valuable or able to be respected. During this time that I visited families, I learned when they have to decide between a man and his children, they choose the man, and the children that are not of that man end up on the streets.

At that moment I understood the importance of educating the women and mainly the girl child. I understood that any change could only be made with education and that is why I decided to create a school only for poor girls — to train future leaders capable of making decisions, become strong women who value themselves, and know when they have to choose between a man and their children, they will make a good decision and not be afraid to face life alone. Why do they learn to say no? Why? I found that for these women life is better IF they accept everything with resignation and submission. This has to change. We must educate women to be capable of facing life with their heads held high and with dignity.

When we went to look for the girls most at risk (girls from single mothers or women vendors who worked on the street with their little ones next to them, or school age girls not in school), we met the women. What they said to us: 'How much will you pay me to take my daughter to your school?' Incredible, but true. They did not think there could be a place or people who without charging anything would educate their daughters, and they thought we had some other interest. This was our experimental beginning while still in Urubamba.

Soon we returned to the Cusco house and began again with one class of 15 girls, the majority from women working, selling snacks in the street. Upstairs our now older boys from the shelter went to the university and studied.

The Urubamba house was sold, and Rae returned to California to raise funds for the school, but the financial situation was critical, and CW had little money. Rae did everything possible in California, but the economic crisis was strong there. My love, Erik, who is always at my side, did everything to support me at this time. And my crazy project suddenly received help from an angel, an anonymous donor. I say angel because for Rae and I nothing is done if the Mother doesn't Love it and SHE sends everything. With the new financial support, we settled in and began working with these new donors sent to help us. I found a bigger building in TupacAmaru, San Sebastian. And we grew class by class to four classes.

When I asked the Mother for help, she sent me Gloria, a woman with a commitment beyond most people, even though, at first, she did not know it — she is a person with a big heart and has grown incredibly. We continued with this support from the anonymous friends of CW who prefer to be unnamed. This financial support built the

152

beautiful school of our dreams. The work of the Mother is always sudden and perfect. Rae and I felt that our dream of providing a quality education in decent conditions with dignity became a reality for our girls.

Efrain says that everything that is given returns in abundance, and he is the one who currently, through his work of guiding tourists, comes to support the foundation as a wonderful son who wants to see change in the future for more girls, like the changes in him."

Gloria Socorro
(Assistant Director, CW School for Girls, Cusco, Peru)

Gloria has worked for Chicuchas Wasi since 1997 as a teaching assistant and earned title of Professor in 2002. From the beginning Gloria had risen quickly to a second lead position.

"I felt that there was something I needed to fill a void in my life. I asked the Divine Mother to guide my way when suddenly Ruth contacted me. She told me about the CW mission and invited me to participate in this beautiful loving family. Without hesitation, I knew that CW was my destiny and I fell in love with the idea.

At first it was very difficult — people did not trust us with their daughters to start kindergarten in a room of the house in Cusco. I remember very well that in the morning the room was a classroom, and in the afternoon, we piled desks to one side of the room and turned it back into a family dining room. Those years were difficult because we were on a tight budget, but we believed in a beautiful dream that our CW school would be different.

Our personal experience of having studied in a public school was that we were just another number in the list of students, and teachers were focused on academics and nothing more. We understood that quality education was important, but there was no concern for the emotional health of students — this is how it still is with public education in my country. In order to make a difference, we understood that comprehensive education was important and needed, and that

153

by combining academics and an improved positive emotional state we would prepare girls to be intelligent women; confident they are capable of making good decisions.

I identify with many of our girls, motherless at a very young age, hoping that in school they will find a loving maternal person — never found in our public schools. CW school is in sharp contrast.

Ruth says, 'Our girls not only look to us as teachers, but we are also like second mothers to give them the love they might not have had in their homes. They respond like loving daughters, and we are so well rewarded. I have no children yet, but when people ask me, I tell them we have 120 daughters and I am very proud of them.'

Ruth taught me to love what we do, and if God and our Divine Mother will let me, I want to continue until the end. Thank you for allowing this beautiful dream to continue to grow."

CHAPTER 17

Changes

> *"To give thanks is to give oneself blessings, to ask all
> the other voices of the ancestors and of the living to
> give you more blessings. We must give thanks, for no
> one's happiness come just from themselves, but from all
> people, ancestral spirits and natural world around you.
> To give thanks means you chose happiness for your life."*
> — Chieftain Chikaka, Shona elder

California-Cusco-California Re-Entry

NEW SMELLS, SOUNDS and visuals overwhelmed me with desire,
passion and memories, still unavailable, but closer. Alone and naked
I faced this new world ready to strip me of what I had left. There is
more. Much more. My baptism had begun. Nothing was familiar, yet
everything was. Every cell was vibrating to some new rhythm. I was
never consulted. Absolute faith carried me through and still does today. My life would never be the same.

Days moved into years, and I have learned to live straddling one
leg in the South and the other in the North. Life presented opportunities to me; I took some and ran from others. Chicuchas Wasi, the children's project, was one of these opportunities. The Urubamba 'Urpi

Wasi' B&B retreat-center (House of Peace) where CW project lived for nine years was another. No holds barred. Blind trust.

Pulled back to the North, I now live again in California. Andean hands now guide CW with me as backup. God has clear plans for us, unseen until they land on us. A happy reunion back in California with my sons and I can see and spend more time with my granddaughters. My Andean daughter, Rosa, lives with me and is on education scholarship in California. The transition back to the USA is difficult otherwise but a little bit of Peru stands at my side; we are two now straddling two continents, one North and one South.

Ruth & Gloria & experimental class in Urubamba 1998

Talented teacher Gloria with her great murals

Ruth & Gloria lead exercise to wake up little ones new to school

1st computer class for CW young kindergarteners.

Oral care class with their first toothbrushes.

Ruth teaches new Quechua speaking child words in Spanish

CW teaching Kindergarten girls class

Rae & Ruth planning CW school expansion to big school

CW NEW primary school opens & fills in rural Cusco

Students learn practical shopping with money management

New kinder girls assigned a big sister, their guide to school

Girls dance at celebration then it's lunch time

Inti Raymi CW INCA history class theater-all students participate

Teacher KarenT instructs her class students

How to vote: Candidate debates,
vote for school Mayor-then teach parents

Young kinder teaches her class how to make quinoa drink

Concentrating on assignment material

Morning assembly in the CW school court yard-all students

Efrain gets a CW LOVE Hugathon moment at the school

Rae gets LOVE Hugathon from girls after meditation

Gloria is creating the CW personal library mural for the girls

6th grade study group

Students work in small groups on a special assignment

Ruth and Rae show new books about equality for everyone

CWhas a huge new Martin Curry library packed with interesting books

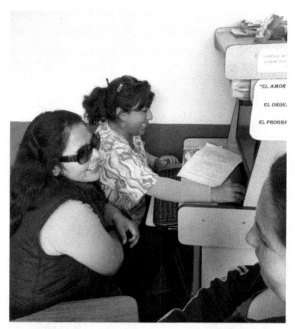

Teachers working on their lessons together

Students teach class subject-teachers watches

Meditation classes for all students during a visit from Rae

Outdoor art class

*CW big 30 years celebration at the school
for parents, staff, visitors and students*

Cross-Cultural Inner Turmoil

When I returned to the states, my shoulders slumped, direction unclear, rules unclear, obedient joining the herd unknown to me, and lost. I wrote, and I wrote, and I wrote; and, finally, I returned to school. I studied computers to learn how to help Chicuchas Wasi organization in this time, and I wrote intensely about the inner collision of my two worlds now back in my country. Words after words filled the pages; images and pain splashed on the paper like a traumatized soda released. They painted a picture. The picture is of me, who I am, where I've been and where I am going. Understanding comes to me slowly. Too slowly! It takes time to process all I have received, maybe a lifetime.

At 3:30 every morning for months I woke up as if an alarm had gone off to respond to some order from inside me to hold the pen and put it on paper. Pages and pages were smeared with ink. When it became light outside, I put the pen down. I filled three 2.5-inch binders in three months. Ideas poured in like steady rain while driving, bathing, talking, reading, and dreaming. There was no choice. It was to write and have peace or don't write and suffer.

My friends would call: *"Rae, what are you doing over there? It's been a week."*

"Writing."

"Writing? What DO you write about for all those hours?"

"Whatever wants to get out"

"Oh, are you ok?"

"Yeah, I'm great, really. Don't worry. It's like school, but an inner school, and I am learning so much."

CHAPTER 18

CW School for Girls Opens in Cusco

"If you want to break the cycle of poverty,
EDUCATE A GIRL." —UNICEF

THE YEAR 1999 is almost over and pushes us all into the 21st Century new millennium. Once more, CW has accomplished much in the past 12 months, including our big location change back to Cusco. Those members of CW at the school are dedicated and work hard, and California is hard at it too— fundraising. We recognize that we can never do all we do alone and are grateful to our many friends and supporters. After 12 years, we are still going strong on little money. We attribute our success to our remarkable team, our CW family spirit, our sound focused simplicity, and the manageable and controlled size of our project.

Moving back to the Cusco house (the temporary headquarters for the first CW kindergarten class in Cusco), we didn't skip a beat. The Peruvian school year ended December 18th at the Urubamba Chicuchas Wasi Alternative School, completing our third and last year bringing the joy of learning to forgotten little girls of Urubamba. Ruth hugged each of our 14 little girls, reminding each one that she was ready to go to public school now, and sent them on their way. The toothless smiles and sparkling eyes she received from the same 14 pairs of eyes, previously dull and vacant, is reward enough for this teacher. Their future has hope. After that everyone was in motion, and all CW furniture and belongings were moved to the newly refurbished Cusco house.

CW Family Routine Takes Shape Once Again

Sopa de Quinoa (Quinoa soup) boils on the stove, and Efrain drops the last potato into the *estafado de pollo* (chicken stew), the midday main meal. It's lunchtime, and Efrain's turn to cook. Efrain, Alejandra (Ruth's one-year-old), Erik, and Ruth sit down hungrily in front of steaming bowls of soup.

Hipolito thunders through the front door, spills his book-filled pack on a chair, and takes his seat at the table. Placing their hands together, a circle is formed, and thanks is given for their many blessings. Eating is serious business here and begins quietly — food is never taken for granted. Hipolito grins from ear to ear, takes a deep breath, and says he did well on his test, his reward for studying day and night – he is determined. Efrain has a group of tourists he must meet at 1:30 to tour the City of Cusco as part of his training. Ruth is tired, but proudly smiles at Hipolito. She spent the morning with administrative red tape at the Ministry of Education closing out the year and school in Urubamba to make ready for next year in Cusco. Erik spent the morning buying supplies, adjusting cabinets and unpacking boxes. The move from Urubamba to Cusco is done. Not an easy move but finished. Little by little, everyone gets comfortable and the dust settles.

After months of preparation, hunting down forgotten little girls tucked away in obscure corners of Cusco and more bureaucratic red tape, CW school begins in Cusco at the start of the Peruvian School year in March 2000.

It is 8:00 a.m. on the first day and only five four-year-olds straggle in, as if just climbing out from under a rock somewhere. The next day there are two more five-year-olds, and then, a few days later, there are 10. The pace is slow and laid back in Cusco, but by November we have 14 *ninas* (girls) ready to end their first kindergarten year in school and all have adjusted to the routine. Dropped off in the morning by older siblings or an occasional parent, they take their seat and wait — all eyes focus on Ruth, their teacher, and School Director. Class time is noisy and quiet, with shy smiles, laughter and sometimes tears. Today, after many months, Jessica spells out her name slowly, deliberately and with her full attention. Covering the gaping holes between the clean white teeth that fill her face, she holds her achievement up for Ruth to see. 'Jessica' is written in big letters and smooth thick strokes on a piece of white paper. Success!

Each morning antsy, squirming bodies form a line for the bathroom: toileting, hand washing and teeth brushing. When all the girls are squeaky clean, they move outside to the patio for fresh air, jumping, and yelling; it's *Recreo* (recess) and patio games for 15 minutes. Soon, happy girls with growling tummies clamber for their seats as white metal mugs of hot oatmeal are placed in front of them along with a warm Cusco-style bread bun on each desk.

Now back to kindergarten basics: a red felt-tip pen slides across the white acrylic board making simple pictures of carrots to teach numbers. This is a typical kindergarten day at CW.

Twelve Years Making a Big Difference!

Chicuchas Wasi School has skipped through the year 2000 with hardly a hiccup. The challenges of Peru's current political chaos: strikes, 6% inflation, less-than-favorable exit of President Fujimori and the missing $8 million this year has moved past us in a flurry, but CW hasn't slowed down one bit. In fact, our project is even more important.

The CW school, located in the center of Cusco, is filled each day with 15 laughing, eager five-year-olds bursting through our door. Professora Ruth Uribe, Director of CW School, quickly scans to see who is missing, and sends her assistant Gloria, or goes herself to get them. Gloria finds them alone at home. Their mothers have forgotten them or just can't be bothered. They are unwashed, unfed and half-asleep. A quick cleanup and they are escorted to class. The late stragglers arrive with giggling eyes, and slide behind their personal desk in time for breakfast. And class begins. Everyday CW teaches reading, writing, arithmetic, history, hygiene, and social skills. After a busy morning together, class ends at 1:00 p.m., and the children are collected by an older brother, sister, mother, or sometimes not at all. Ruth knows where to find the mother of those abandoned, or the names and location of the *tias* (motherly women) also working in the market who look after certain children when the mother has proven unreliable).

Most of our young students have little parental support or supervision. Most are daughters of single mothers working in the open market from a blanket of produce spread out on the ground — the only way they know to scrape together pennies for their survival. Little girls are often left home alone to do chores until their mother returns at night, or they too work in the market. Their unskilled mothers, desperate for survival, look to any man to provide for them. They see no other option. These casual *tios*, (male friends of the mothers) are called uncles, usually don't work, and are frequently drunk and belligerent, and dislike these children born of other men. The following scenario is of one of our students, but there are others much worse.

Chelita lives with her mother in a barrio, (neighborhood), on a hill behind the plaza in Cusco. Her mother leaves her alone every morning to sell her bundle of carrots in the market usually returning late, often with a tio, and often drunk and rowdy, oblivious to her young daughter. The tio grumbles unintelligible words and pushes her mother around and onto the floor. He shouts at her, she cries, they both cry while Chelita hides in terror. The loud voices eventually turn to whimpers and lovemaking, while Chelita huddles on the dirt floor against the wall under the bed. Early the next morning, the mother and tio leave, hung-over and unkempt, and oblivious to the small child still hiding under the bed. Chelita is left once more to fend for herself.

About that time, Ruth knocks on the open front door. No-one answers. She peers into the one-room dark adobe at a messed-up single bed, two chairs and a wooden table; there are no toys or other furnishings. Entering, she sees there is no visible food anywhere and no fire in the fogon (stove) in the corner, an Andean style rammed mud stove. Experience has taught her too well and she knows what has taken place; she looks for Chelita under the bed. Coaxing her out, Ruth speaks soft words in Quechua to the sad-eyed rag doll before her, while brushing off the dirt and wrinkles pressed into her clothes and hair. The short walk under the warm sun to CW school recharges Chelita's spirits, and a smile of anticipation slowly spreads across her face as she marches next to her beloved teacher.

These are the children who make up the Chicuchas Wasi School and we are committed to giving them at least basic tools for survival. From our class of 1999, six students entered the public school system — something their own mothers had never achieved. We work with the Peruvian Ministry of Education to bring these overlooked girl children up to a level where they are able to pass the public school entry exam and continue with their education. Others continue with us when their challenges are greater. Our students gain skills intended to lift them from hopelessness and despair to a future where they have choices. We change every child, every day, every minute. We continue to reeducate their mothers as to their value as females and the importance of educating their daughters.

CW Shelter Young Adults Excel at the University

Efrain and Hipolito, our incredible rising stars, were living on the streets when CW first gave them shelter in 1987. Now, as young adults fending for themselves alone in our Cusco house the last year, both have had their noses buried in university textbooks. Hipolito, 20, is majoring in Business Economics, and Efrain, 22, in Tourism; and both are doing well. Rosa graduated from Ursuline High School two years ago and was accepted to Sonoma State University in California. She is in her sophomore year, majoring in Computer Science, but beginning to lean toward Nursing. She is under partial scholarship and working as I am to help keep her there and making us all proud. Happily, the CW family is together again under the same roof in Cusco and Rosa is living with Rae in California, buried in her studies as well.

The challenge of the still-present political chaos, the Peruvian monetary devaluation adjustments and the 5.5 inflation rate has not slowed down in Peru at all in the year 2000 and is shrinking the value of the dollars I raise for our $15,000-$18,000 yearly budget since we must convert USD to Peruvian Soles.

CW School Achievements

Another day in class, students quickly settle at their personal desks, focused on Profesora Ruth — ready for today's first lesson. She looks at each one, in the eye, commanding that their heads are held up and eyes off the floor. It's show-and-tell time. *"Quen tiene algo para compartir hoy?"* (What do you have to share today?) She asks, and all hands are instantly up in the air.

Our spirits are up, and Ruth reports our classes are open every day and filled with the enthusiasm of little girls excited that THEY get to go to school. We have had a number of false starts and frustrations with the transportation strikes and political chaos in the last six months. Hewlett-Packard has finally arrived from Lima with our shining six new computers and the peripheral hardware to install them all today. A common thread to remember is that time in Peru has no relation to time in California, as I know it. Here slow is too slow for me and the California slow would be too fast for people here. Nothing happens with ease and everything is an effort. So, we all learn to take a deep breath and relax. We began plans for our little computer lab in 1995 and finally we will be able to install them today in 2000 in an upstairs available bedroom. In Cusco people march to the beat of a different rhythm that prioritizes family and social time, children's time and then comes business.

The never-ending saga of official obstacles continues to bombard Ruth, and the latest is the new mayor's decision to rescind the property tax exemption awarded to CW in 1998, and he intends to collect the back taxes from then to today. This is not new behavior, and we won't let it happen, but it keeps Ruth busy. CW has been blessed with a lawyer in the family. Ruth's husband Erik now handles the countless meetings to prove that our documents are valid, in order, and that we have complied with all the requirements. These are never-ending attempts to fill empty pots with US green. We usually always triumph, but to maintain our focus on the children in class everyday means we must step over these boulders as they fall before us. Ruth is born, raised and educated in Cusco and stands tall to plow right through the slightly corrupt bureaucratic red tape. Her skill shows, and she never skips a class.

CW Family Grows in 2001

Ruth and her husband Erik have started their family. Director / Teacher Ruth delivered her second child, Paula, in 2000, a companion for her sister Alejandra born in 1998, now two years old. Mom and babies are healthy. Babies in hand, she still teaches her students.

I have been reflecting on our 1987 humble beginnings offering emergency shelter to abandoned street children, and safety to so many children who came through our doors during the 10 years of the CW Shelter. My heart is filled with loving memories of these kind yet wild kids. We still guide and support three exceptional young adults from the early years who have surpassed Ruth's and my expectations. These two boys have achieved well academically and have developed into deep-thinking conscious young men of impeccable integrity. Efrain is now 23 years old, a Professional Cusco Tour Guide and has begun a one-year internship. Hipolito, now 20, is at the University of Cusco with two years of a major in Business Economics, and neck – deep in finals – our street urchins turned scholars. Both young men are serious students, kindhearted gentlemen, and offer quiet understanding and affection to the CW girls while offering help to Ruth in the school when time allows. Rosa, also 20, is in her second year at Sonoma State University, California, her 6th year studying in the USA, and has just changed her major to Nursing. She wants to be a Nurse Practitioner, and her enthusiasm and serious focus is impressive. She has mastered English and doing very well. We at CW look at these three achievers, knowing the obstacles they have had to overcome to get where they are today, in absolute awe. We are honored to have done our part and to have made such a difference with all who have linked arms with us in our effort to educate and support these shining examples of humanity.

CHAPTER 19

Still Fundraising
After All These Years — 2002

*"When we liberate girls with an education, they liberate
those around them."* — Queen Rania of Jordan

FOR THE LAST 14 years we have raised the funds needed to operate CW, possible since we had no administrative overhead, due to
the in-kind donations from our professionally-skilled and talented
California CW Board of Directors, friends and supporters via garage
sales, Peruvian folk art sales, Andean music concerts, my travel tours
to Peru, the *'Urpi Wasi B&B'*, and monies collected from 4th grade
classroom projects in the USA, and your donations. A $20.00 dona-
tion does matter, and feeds all 20 students a hot oatmeal breakfast
for four days at CW. We have, and are still, changing the grim future
that these forgotten little girls would face without the basic education, empowerment and preparation they receive at CW for a future
of honorable work, personal safety, and to be positive role models for
their future children. Together with many who believe educating girls
matters a lot, we are reinventing the story of the powerless/helpless
impoverished female in Peru.

Ruth and I talk on the phone two to three times a week, if not more, for moral support for us both. Ruth is stretching the dollar as much as possible and I am trying to raise more dollars so that we can rent a bigger location. Until we get more space to expand, every year we still prepare 15 to 20 little girls to be promoted from our school, ready to take the entrance exam required to enter public school... and 95% pass. They are out of the kitchen, off the clothes washboard, or caring for siblings long enough to learn the initial basic 3Rs. They will need to defend themselves economically too soon. We have won the respect and support of uneducated parents who once believed that educating girls was a waste of time. Now they push and pull in the long registration line from our front door to the street to get their daughter, niece, or goddaughter enrolled into Chicuchas Wasi School.

We are still grassroots today with no frills, but we have what we need. With 98% of our donations going directly to the school, this is an opportunity to show how we used our annual budget of $20,000 in 2002:

- Ruth Uribe - 1 teacher/director salary, health benefits, retirement per law
- Gloria Vera - 1 assistant teacher salary, health, etc. per Peruvian law
- Free quality education for 20 little girls in our school
- Unannounced follow-up home visits and constantly connecting with parents
- All school materials, uniforms and supplies provided for every student
- A prepared classroom; a personal desk for each student, and a computer lab to expose the students with special introductory age-related classes.
- Brain food: hot oatmeal breakfast for all girls, and a hot meal mid-day, aware most girls are poorly malnourished at home
- CW is the liaison for girls to gain entrance to the public school

system, providing initial uniform, notebooks, pencils and as-
sistance to the parents.

- CW is active member of the community participating in all
the parades, festivals and educational presentations of Cusco.
- Obligatory parent classes emphasizing their daughter's potential, teaching the value of educating girls, women's rights, and
personal self-worth. Psychologist works with girls and parents
in class and privately as needed.

Little Known Strategy Used by Large Foundations

In 2002 and 2003, it was near impossible to obtain financial support for a small project like ours because big numbers of enrollees
count — success rate is seldom asked for, and Peru was not politically popular with donors. We know that Bigger is NOT better; we
have seen first-hand the many land cruisers and high standard living
of staff paid by some of these same organizations in Peru. We have
demonstrated our fantastic results, received favorable remarks, but
still organizations behind the big desks with the funding want big
numbers — to spend big.

We have continued to sell Peruvian folk art anywhere we can,
send out newsletter requests for donations, have open house gatherings to introduce donors to Ruth when in California with some improvement, but in 2002 and 2003, the US economy was tight. I had
to return to a nursing job to support Rosa and I in California — post
retirement.

Ruth has successfully called on the support of friends, professional contacts and family in the Cusco community for free care for her
students when they need medical or psychological help, and dental
treatments, as well as free class trips to the zoo and museums. As
Ruth puts it: *"With the support from my friends and family, if one of
the children needs a dental or medical treatment I can get it donated,
but what I cannot get in my country is financial help."*

184

CHAPTER 20

New Boulders Upset Our Path

"Too often we underestimate the power of a touch, a kind word, a listening ear, an honest compliment, or the smallest act of caring, all of which have the potential to turn a life around." — Leo Buscaglia

IN MARCH 2003, school opened as usual with a typical new and promising student, Milagros. The only female and youngest of four siblings entered the classroom for the first time. Prior to attending CW, Milagros's mother left her alone while she searched for work as a *lavandera* (washer of someone else's dirty clothes). Some days she is lucky and earns enough to buy food for her family. Milagros's brothers go to school, while four-year-old Milagros is left home abandoned, hungry, and dirty. A prevailing belief in the higher intelligence of the male child over the female child in the uneducated community is a big obstacle to education of girls.

Ruth is a Cusco-born teacher/director of CW, uses her well-honed skill and finds Milagros hiding behind a table. Together they obtain the mother's permission for Milagros to attend school, but only because Ruth promises to feed her, food being more valued than female education. Her mother frequently fails to retrieve her when school is out at 1:30 p.m., finally arriving at 9:00 p.m., well after dark, for her little daughter, with excuses Ruth has learned to accept. Milagros's mother will soon realize and appreciate her daughter's growth and learning, but at first it is always the same — the mothers see no point in educating a girl who should be washing and cooking at home.

These are still difficult times with many tugs on donor wallets. Ruth and I trust that the hand that has always guided us will also do so again now. CW is changing forever the unbearable reality of at least 20 little girls this year, their siblings, cousins, and parents every year. We keep our budget tight and our classroom doors open together with the donations of generous people who believe all children need education. We have been blessed and I know we will continue to be.

CW is more than a school. While preparing our girls to enter the public school system, we have encountered serious problems in the home. These little girls often witness their mothers being raped by their fathers, husbands, brother-in-laws, etc. Frustrated mothers routinely beat their children, lacking any other outlet for their sense of helplessness and anger. The children pay for this and repeat the behavior with their own children. We have expanded our parent classes — a requirement for all parents in our school where we teach the parents better ways to cope in difficult moments and support their child's development. This parent education results in mothers who are learning to respect and protect their daughters.

One single mother, Janet, worked as a domestic and was raped at 17 by the man of the house. She discovered she was pregnant, and birthed Rosita who is now six and in our school. Rosita has been rejected from many schools due to her aggressive and violent behavior. When Ruth originally refused to take Rosita, the frustrated and violent mother told Ruth she wanted to kill her child since all her problems started when Rosita was born. Ruth's lawyer husband guided CW, and the children's judge intervened to protect the child. Rosita continues under the watchful eyes of Ruth at CW.

The children we work with usually receive no affection or tenderness from their mothers, because the mothers have never received it themselves. CW works with these children, their mothers, and 30%

of the fathers who participate in our school, to teach the power of demonstrating love and affection. Their children come to school fighting to hug Ruth and their mothers thank her.

Eighteen years have gone by and today we have gained the trust of this community of poor uneducated families. They now come to Ruth begging to register their daughters and sharing their deepest secrets and personal problems. We are finding that many of these mothers are so psychologically damaged that they don't know what they want or need and make bad decisions, putting their children at risk. Often the children are blamed for their condition and inability to change the situation — poverty, loneliness, alcohol, and financial dependency — on any available male. Some fathers are also frustrated and want to change. These are some of the hard-to-hear stories of the real lives that the community we serve struggle with and why CW is needed. There is no one else to help them. We have become social workers as well as teachers.

2004 Hard Times

In spite of hard times everywhere, somehow CW has somehow managed to keep its doors open yet another year. We have seriously tightened our belt in 2004 but we continue one day at a time, stay small and manageable; but this year is incredibly tough and the California CW Board of Directors needs to have a bittersweet conversation with Ruth in person.

In September I returned to Cusco to discuss our limited options with Ruth. The mothers, fathers, and children welcomed me with their dances, stories, and enthusiasm as a thank you for the opportunity to achieve beyond the kitchen and dirty laundry. Seventeen five-year-olds dressed in their typical red costumes and danced, twirled, and stamped their feet to the fast Cusquena rhythm for their parents and me. Big glistening eyes revealed pure joy and their pride.

One mother presented me with a beautiful hand-carved wooden

jewelry box and a framed photo of this class as a thank you. One clap of the hands from Ruth, our director, and a loud shuffle of feet and the children lined up for another dance. Two uniformed graduates from last year joined the line of dancers representing earlier CW students now enrolled in the public school to express gratitude for their preparation making it possible.

Chicuchas Wasi has achieved much since we opened our doors in 1987. We have helped hundreds of children in small numbers improve their lives since then. Our school continues to offer opportunities to forgotten little girls preparing them to learn to read and write and basic math. They will no longer be destined to follow in the shoes of the mothers — unable to provide for themselves. They know about school now. They can now gain entry to public school with confidence and self-esteem.

Each year we receive 20 children rejected by the public education system, unable to meet basic entry requirements. We prepare them academically, and their parents to value their daughters who are intelligent and who can be independent adults one day. We once had to seek out these little girls hidden away behind stoves and caring for younger siblings, but no longer. When school begins, mothers and aunties form long lines at our door to register, sadly we must turn away many.

Still, we have prepared more than 160 little girls to be able to pass public school entry tests.

CW Faces Closure

Early in 2004 we seriously tightened our belt, cut all overhead and one part time assistant — leaving our Director/Teacher alone. With only Ruth to administer and teach, we still managed to continue with daily classes for 12 little girls who we could not abandon; their need was so great. Our two older boys from CW's earlier shelter, Efrain and Hipolito, and Ruth's husband Erik have all helped enormously and prevented our school from closing. Again, I say with great pride, surmounting all obstacles, we continue to have incredible success to change the future for the poor little girls of Cusco and their parents. But we could not continue like this... Ruth was tired.

Chicuchas Wasi faced hard times that seem insurmountable and with harder decisions. Our funds had all but dried up; donors haad declined. While in Peru we discussed the closing of our project with a heavy heart. Our adult graduates of the Shelter, Efrain and Hipolito, spoke emotionally about how the CW family gave them a home and education and changed their future. They wanted to help other children have the same opportunity and agreed to join forces with Ruth to make this happen. Efrain spoke to his new wife about giving up their new apartment to return to the CW house and school and use their rent money instead to help fund the school. As you can see, these are our passionate CW beneficiaries who know first-hand the value of our work. They will stand by CW and its future any way they can. What amazing young men. Ruth and I were unable to move past our sadness and needed to go to California for any lifeline that might have appeared and have a serious conversation with the CA BOD. Since I am the main fundraiser and have been fretting for the last year, they will not be surprised. The bittersweet reality the school faced hung heavy over my heart. I was waiting for Ruth to come and meet with the board of directors about this sad ending of our successful work. She came, and we told our stories, tried to hold our tears but the dam couldn't hold. There was no solution. No magic wand.

Divine Mother Is Always Near

During Ruth's return trip, I received a telephone call from an old friend asking if she might share my name and phone number with her old college friend who wants to do something similar to CW in Cusco. I said yes, of course. But sadness engulfed me.

Minutes later, the call came from her friend, to remain anonymous, and we talked a long time. I made suggestions for her on how to start her project, never mentioned CW as I was grieving our loss; I just didn't think to do that. After realizing that she would actually need to live with her new project in Cusco to get it started and staffed — this cannot be done by just sending money — she asked me about CW. It was then I realized she was interested in helping CW. She requested the documents, budget, etc. to vet us and to determine how interested she was. She soon called back, donated the annual budget and donated the funds to rent a larger building. Gratitude was not a big enough word. CW had a year to think of some new way to stay afloat. I have never questioned a greater wisdom and knew this was the blessing of the Mother. I called Ruth immediately and we were both in shock at the divine intervention from the Mother.

We grew out of the Cusco house, but had gained a foothold and a reputation for a special success at our school. Our little girls were showing their smarts everywhere. So, we expanded to a rental building just south of the Cusco Plaza and we squeezed in four grades in the next few years as girls were promoted to the next grade.

Fundraising ideas began to appear, people asked if they could go with me to Peru on my next visit, and I organized a group tour that helped fund part of the budget. Efrain began to bring his tour groups to the school, and they donated to Ruth directly or sent donations to me later. The anonymous woman became more active with some of her friends during visits to the school.

For the next few years the Chicuchas Wasi School for Girls continued happily with many more girls enrolled and we were making big inroads in the community about the value of education for girls.

Our Stars from the CW Shelter

Remember Hipolito, 25, one of our shining stars? He was due to graduate in Business Accounting from the University of Cusco last year, but the six-month-long strike closed the University. Just now in October 2005, the last strike is over. Hopefully he will graduate soon.

Our second shining star, Efrain, 28, graduated 2002 in Tourism, married last year and is expecting his first child in April, 2006. These young men entered CW when we offered them emergency shelter from the dangers of living on the streets, and a home. Both boys plan to carry forward the work of CW as soon as their lives are settled. They both help now as often as possible.

Also, Rosa, now 25, just graduated from Sonoma State University-School of Nursing in California. She is scheduled to take her state exam soon. She came to California on a full ride scholarship at 14 years old, graduated from Ursuline High School, and received partial grant to SSU. Our young adults are ready to begin their adult lives now. Efrain, a director on the Peru Board, is an amazing ambassador for CW school. Rosa, a director on the California CW Board, helps to manage the CW Facebook posts.

CHAPTER **21**

Chicuchas Wasi School Pushes Forward

"Make of yourself a light." — Buddha

CW SCHOOL IS growing yearly in the larger rented location and has survived the economic crisis. Over the years since we opened our school for girls, we have served many children living with a variety of realities. You have already read enough of these difficult and tragic stories to understand the importance of CW School for Girls to change the future for girls and end the sad reality of uneducated women trapped in poverty, oppression, physical and sexual abuse and more. Without CW these girls will inherit the life of the women who came before them. We are breaking this chain and empowering girls to be future leaders for change in Cusco society for gender equality. For more than 23 years Chicuchas Wasi organization has provided much to the children of Cusco and in just the 13 years of our CW School, serving 66 girls in 2010 and 92 girls by 2012, we easily have more than enough stories to create another book.

Chicuchas Wasi Challenge, Reality and Success at a Glance

The day begins at 6:00 a.m. for Ruth. She is up, dressed and rushing her two daughters through breakfast and getting ready for school. By 7:10 the family is out the door and down the 60 or so stairs to retrieve the CW van from the garage down the street. Ruth, her daughters and the three or four CW students just arriving hustle inside the van and they are off to CW school, dropping off Ruth's daughters at their school in route. By 7:20 the older first and second grade students are at their desks beginning their first lesson. Younger students arrive at 8:15 when the first bell rings. Everyone sings the national anthem, recites the Morning Prayer, and then shares important events. Ending the assembly, Ruth leads the warm-up exercise to wake up sleepy brains and cold bodies. Cusco mornings are cold and there is no heat other than the sun. All students split off to their assigned classroom seats and are ready for their teachers by 8:40. The bell rings at 10:00 when the first group of the youngest students breaks for lunch (oatmeal and bread or lentil and rice). They arrive hungry, unable to stay awake or study with growling tummies. There is time to play on the swings, slide or bars, and then it's back to class by 10:30. The bell sounds again for the second lunch group, thus beginning the process again. Fed and ready to learn, all students are back at their desks and at their lessons by 11:00 a.m. All grades are busy with lessons until 12:30 when mothers come to collect the younger students. Older students continue class until 1:30 when they too are picked up. Ruth is off to collect her daughters from their school by 1:45 and deliver the few students she transports. She is home for the main family meal by 3:00 p.m.

Special classes are inserted into the week such as hygiene instruction and oral care using the toothbrush, combs, soap and water action. Today our girls take pride in their appearance; they are clean, teeth and hair brushed, hands washed, and they are wearing clean school uniforms. Before CW, they understood little about hygiene, nor did they care about their appearance.

The girls also sit at a computer keyboard, two at a time, play educational games on the computer — as if they have always done so.

They respond to their teacher's questions with heads high and a voice loud and strong. When they were new to CW their eyes were on the ground and only low mumbling could be heard.

Parents attend the CW parenting classes and school festivals to celebrate their daughters. Before CW nothing like this existed for these families. They lived in isolation.

Some of what I have shared in this book is not visible at the school, but the reality that we have come to understand is too big a burden for our little girls, and we are doing something about that. No social services exist in Cusco or social workers, sadly.

As soon as you enter the school grounds you are engulfed in the love and joy from the girls. They are incredibly demonstrative with their teachers, administrative team and visitors as well. I am surrounded with hugs and bodies wiggling with glee around me when I visit. CW school is an environment where love fills the very air that we all breathe and blasts our hearts wide open. Come visit us and experience the magic that fills CW.

Daily we see our little girls with big, ear-to-ear smiles as they show us, and the community, just how smart they are. In the early years of the CW School for Girls, it took some talking to convince their parents that these young girls were worth educating and it took even longer for the community to see our students' value. Today, after one or two years with us, our girls pass the public school entry exam with the highest scores. They proudly march in all the Cusco parades in their red uniforms with the CW logo, led by our Chicuchas Wasi banner. The community has taken notice.

Since we opened our School for Girls, we have served many children living with a variety of difficult realities — you have heard about several of their histories over the past years. Today we are filled with pride and much emotion when we look back on so much good work completed. We regularly follow up on our graduates, and learn that not only have they advanced academically, but also — and most importantly — they have advanced socially and emotionally, with an improved self-image that strengthens their relationships with family and their community. We can say that the seeds we have planted have sprouted — this truth reflected in the changes noted from where we started with these children, AND their parents (parents who are now aware and committed to a bright future for their daughters) having discovered their daughters' value.

The little girls we serve are hugely in need of special help in addition to basic academics. They come to us with eyes cast down, afraid to make contact, withdrawn and lacking joy. After some time with us the change is notable; eyes sparkle with intelligence, personalities show, and they grow and become stronger emotionally.

Examples of CW Impact

Typical of our girls is Estrella, who depends on her uneducated and unprepared mother for her needs. Her lazy, unprepared and delinquent father is absent. CW seeks to find the best possible solution for the difficult situations affecting each child and family. It is not an easy process. Estrella entered CW kindergarten and today is in 5th grade in high school, working part-time and doing well. Her mother is irresponsible and desperate with four children to feed, all from different absent fathers. When Estrella displeases her mother, she threatens to send her daughter to live with her drunken abusive father of whom she is terrified. Finally, the mother abandoned Estrella and moved to the jungle. CW noticed something was wrong and investigated. A grandmother was located and took charge of the grandchild she loved and to whom she gave a stable home.

Esperanza came to CW as a five-year-old and today is in her second year of high school. She lives with her mother and grandmother. Her grandmother loves her and takes responsibility for her. The mother demands money from the grandmother and threatens to disappear with the child, so the grandmother pays and lives in constant worry and fear. CW works with both in the CW parent class and the relationship is improving. The mother found work and was better until she became pregnant from a casual contact. CW is keeping an eye on this situation.

Felicity joined CW at six years old and today is in her second year of high school. She is from a poor and troubled family. Her father is resentful, abusive and constantly insulting her older sister, his partner's daughter by another man. This came up in the parent class and CW was able to help the family relationship. The mother developed fainting spells due to so much stress and worry for her daughters. Finally, the father found work in a nearby village and relocated the family there. Felicity transferred to another school and is doing well. The mother and Felicity came to visit Ruth and to thank CW for the intervention and to report on her academic achievement.

Over the last few years our enrollment numbers grew rapidly filling every one of the three classrooms with 38 students. In 2009 we added another classroom enrolling 48 students, and in 2010 it was 66 students. Our style of empowerment education for the student and the entire family has so impressed the involved families that soon they overwhelmed our Director, Ruth Uribe, with a plea to add second grade to allow those completing first grade to continue on to second grade with CW. Past years required a transfer to a public school with an entrance exam. We were making so much progress academically and with empowerment that Ruth added 2nd grade in 2009. By the time 2011 rolled around, we had managed to stuff two more grades into the rented building with the whisper that Ruth's CW school dream would soon be a reality. Seventy-five students were being prepared for the new school due to open in 2012.

Since 2015 CW has a staff psychologist who organizes and runs the parent meetings, guides CW Staff and is on call 24/7 on his cell for the CW alumnae. The improvement is stunning.

Today, Chicuchas Wasi girls are marching ahead. 100% continue in school, in different state education centers, and it is no surprise that our girls are academically successful.

We often invite the alumnae girls of Chicuchas Wasi School to our meetings, along with their parents, to come and share their stories with new students and their parents. The new parents learn that with CW these graduate girls have begun a process of growth and change touched by Chicuchas Wasi faith in them and generosity toward their families. This positive influence has spread to the community outside the walls of our school to where these girls and their families live.

CHAPTER **22**

Dreams DO Come True

"It's only with the heart that one can see rightly,
what is essential is invisible to the eye."
—The Little Prince

RUTH STILL HAD a dream that one day our community of impoverished girls would have a school of their own forever and we focused on that dream for years. We held that image in our hearts, and, in a few years, it began to manifest through the generosity and kindness of an anonymous European group who funded the construction of the beautiful CW Primary School. Our unbelievable dream manifested when CW purchased land on the south side of Cusco and built the CW school with room for nine classrooms, K-6. This is Peru and the code word is SLOW, so we knew we must be patient while all the legal, permits, and inspections were made, and insure that no strikes appear to put a stop on building until over. We broke ground in 2010 with a few delays due to rain. etc., but opened in 2012 with all grades through the 5th. The final 6th grade for Peruvian primary school was added in 2013.

We have proven, year after year, that our school fills a need in this community and now we will be able to expand the services we offer. We will forever be grateful to our generous donors, both long-term and new friends, who believe and value education for poor girls. We still need your faith and your financial support so we can continue to offer FREE educational services to all our Chicuchas Wasi School girls.

The European donors who have seen and felt the success of our work have demonstrated their trust in us with this incredible gift for the girls we serve. Our once-forgotten girls will have their own CW Primary School for Girls that will always be there for them.

The Quechua name for the CW School for Girls is *MAMANCHISWAN PURISUNCHIS* in Quechua (*Walking with the Mother*) that the families we serve all understand and value. The name we will use in the USA or Europe will be the CW School for Girls so as not to confuse people who struggle to say the Quechua name of Chicuchas Wasi (the children's project).

During the CW Primary School construction period, Ruth was busy; she had to acquire workers, create plans, gather equipment to make the entry road and other building site preparations. Adobes were made immediately for the security fencing and there were always more government documents to be filed. This was quite an adventure. The beautiful CW Primary School for Girls that we have today is our dream come true. Never doubt the LOVE of the Mother.

Our Beautiful New Primary School

Chicuchas Wasi has blossomed into a full-sized, fully accredited primary school, now located in the rural south end of the Cusco City. The big surprise was the amazing commitment of the anonymous donors who provided the resources to build this beautiful school. At CW this was a long-held dream come true!

By 2012, we had 92 enthusiastic students in seven classrooms ranging from two kindergarten classes, and 1st through 5th grade in our NEW CW primary school. In 2013 we added a 6th grade, the final class to complete the Chicuchas Wasi Alternative Primary

School for Girls, for marginalized girls of this region. We have hovered around 123 to 130 students since with the addition of the new class and more kindergartners. Our generous donors who built this full primary school are the CW Angels, and we thank you for your faith in us over the years and your financial support so we can continue to offer FREE educational services to all our Chicuchas Wasi School girls.

Here is what Celeste, one of our students, had to say:

"I was born in Chumbivilcas, in the year 2004. My birthday is March 15, and I am eight years old. My father's name is Jose, and he works on the farm. My mom is Rebeca. We are 11 siblings, and I am the last. My mommy took care of us, but the trouble was that my dad beat my mom and she could not stand it and died and left me only a baby. I had no one to look after me — my dad did not want me, or feed me, or dress me, so I feel very sad. I was given to my aunt, and now I am with her. Initially I lived with her mother and she hit me and didn't take care of me or want me. But my teacher Ruth spoke to my aunt, and now she takes care of me, loves me and I am happy — happy because I have a family. I am very mischievous and make problems for myself because of my mischief. I am very happy to be in this school of Chicuchas Wasi because they love me a lot and forgive me when I misbehave. I never want to go away from here."

Our Parents Have Learned of their Importance at the CW School.

Like all schools in Peru, Chicuchas Wasi unleashes Peruvian pride with flags flying and all students, teachers, parents and guests stand assembled and sing the national anthem. CW celebrates The Day of Cusco with many special activities. Mothers of our girls dance typical Cusco dances in full costume for the crowd of onlookers visiting our school for the fiesta. Tasty typical dishes are sold to hungry buyers, by each classroom— fun and lip-smacking everywhere.

Proud parents have been drawn successfully into the CW program with active participation and desire to learn about their daughters and hopes for less struggle in their future.

The mothers of our students create and organize an interesting contest as a competition between the individual classrooms. The mothers of each class prepare traditional dishes from the three areas of Peru: the jungle, the coast and the mountains. Each class sets up a table to present these dishes for sale, and in this way earn money for something their classroom needs. The class demonstrating the best effort wins a special prize.

There are many learning opportunities in this event. The home-room mother from each class presents a budget to the CW school director, Ruth Uribe, who then loans each class the money needed to buy the ingredients to make the dishes. The mothers of each class prepare the food together and then sell servings to the public during the fiesta. Proceeds from the sale of food by each classroom first go to pay back the loan, and the resulting profit goes to the classrooms. Every class participates and the classroom with the tastiest dish also gets a prize.

Last year the mothers earned enough money with food sales that they were able to buy each class a DVD player to use with previous-ly-donated TVs for viewing special educational videos in classrooms. Most of our mothers are active in the school and take their turn seri-ously as lead room-mothers organizing the other mothers in any way needed to assist the teachers. They do this for their daughters whom they are watching blossom like flowers.

CHAPTER 23

My Passion

(by Ruth Uribe, CW School Creator, Administrator)

"Every child deserves a champion – an adult who will never give up on them, who understands the power of connection and insists that they become the best that they can possibly be." —Rita Pierson

"THE GREATEST GIFT in life is to have the opportunity to live and share our experiences. Not everyone is able to feel what is special about our girls at Chicuchas Wasi School for Girls.

Each girl comes to our school with her history reflected in her face; there is fear, anguish and sadness. Our mission is to restore her inner joy and help her find strength to face life with courage and love.

For us, each girl is her own universe that we must respect and help her to develop. It is so important to care for her emotional, social, biological and intellectual development, which we incorporate into our program. However, we receive many girls who bring with them very deep wounds.

Generally, our girls bring emotional wounds as most come from dysfunctional families. We have girls who live with a caretaker that is not family, or a single mother, an aunt, or both parents. Most of them are filled with abusive anger and don't communicate or give them *love. This might not be due to a lack of desire or intention, but due to ignorance (ignorance as not understanding something unknown to them), so you cannot easily blame when we need to open not only the minds of our girls and parents, but also their hearts.*

CW will have its first graduating class this year 2013 from our primary school. We feel this is our first big achievement for CW School, even though we know that our work is constant, and we have to begin again each year, each day, and each moment. Today our girls, as you have already read some of their shared stories, are girls who will break the vicious cycle of violence and anger, submission and sadness. Because their transformation has not only been external, with a good education, nice uniforms, nutritious food, but also with personal inner healing. They have replaced resentment and fear with forgiveness and joy and have acquired newly earned confidence to realize their dreams."

2013 Was Our First Graduation Class In The New Primary School

What makes this year so special is that we graduated our first 6th grade class with students who have been with us since kindergarten. That means they have had the benefit of the Chicuchas Wasi style of quality primary education created especially for them, ignored and unvalued in their communities.

We have seen the changes in girls who entered CW School at four or five years of age with no hope for a positive future. As the years went by, these same girls began to light up with energy, interest and promise, becoming so bright there was no question of their inner healing and hope for tomorrow. As graduation nears, these same girls are ecstatic about their personal growth and achievements and their joy is contagious.

For Ruth and I and the teachers, all dedicated to helping our girls utilize the opportunities provided to them at CW, we are extremely proud of their achievements and development. A bright light is shining over CW and on our students.

In rural areas, every grade level student receives a diploma at the end of each school year to prove that they were promoted to the next level. They are very proud to receive their diploma from Ruth. Educating Girls could not be more urgent than it is today.

The high spirits of these graduating students have infected the younger classmates who can now see their own future in the eyes of our 6th graders about to move on. It is bittersweet to see them leave, but we know they are well prepared to confront the world and their futures.

With the blessing of our new CW full primary school just completed, our annual budget just jumped to $131,000 for the new primary school. With 120 girls projected and eight teachers, plus the two teachers in administration, a secretary, chauffeur, cooks, and security, we must rethink how we fundraise once again.

California Board of Directors 2017

*CW School bus driver, teachers, cooks,
secretary and Psychologist in Cusco*

*Assist. Dir. Gloria began as 18 yr. old student teacher
in 1998 with CW*

CW family with Ruth, Erik, Hipolito, Efrain and families and Rae

Efrain, Sonia and his children today

Hipolito, Janet and his daughters

Hipolito & Efrain grew up in CW, are professional men today

*Rosa grew up in CW, Professional Nurse
in California and mother today*

Rosa and1year old son Julien

Ruth, Erik and girls: Alejandra and Paula

Ruth and Rae in 2012 – United Vision for 30 years

CW parents plant & harvest veggies they grow for the school

CW Christmas and graduation with staff honoring graduates

Gloria, Rae & Ruth feeling great about CW success

Creative Fundraising Once Again

Upon learning of the new school budget, I took a big breath and went online to investigate new creative forms of fundraising and I discovered Crowd Funding and gave it a try. Small nonprofits not blessed with a big endowment fund must always keep one eye on the changes in fundraising for the times. Crowd funding was pretty new, and I think we entered at the right time. Over the years we became well known and drew in more donors than I could have done alone with an email. However, the learning curve is pretty wide, involving online classes, groups, and webinars to gain more know-how. I put the word out in a newsletter asking friends and donors for ideas and organizations they might have knowledge of and was so happy to hear from you all. All those extra eyes and ears were such a big help to me that year.

This was the year that our impressive ambassador and CW board member, Efrain Valles, began working full time in tourism and bringing most of his tourists to visit the school. He has single-handedly helped us increase our funding for the operating budget of the new school. As part of the CW family for 30 years, he knew better than most the value of our mission to educate girls. What would we do without him?

First Alumnae Sisterhood Group Forms

The Chicuchas Wasi School for girls graduated another outstanding class of 6th graders in December of 2014. Ruth came up with a great idea to keep in touch with prior students. She created the CW Alumnae Sisterhood Group to keep our girls in contact with CW once out the nest, and also to share their experiences with the new grads. No meeting with teenagers is complete without food and laughter, and both were present.

Our excited, but anxious, new grads were relieved to talk with the now experienced CW alumnae to help prepare them for the reality of public school. The CW Alumnae students told high school stories and gave advice to the new CW grads about the transition from their beloved CW school to a co-ed public high school. This gathering of our alumnae students is a new CW program to build alumnae sisterhood and allow Ruth to get follow-up reports on the girls going forward. The first sisterhood meeting of the combined 2013, 2014 and now 2015 alumnae girls met over lunch in Ruth's home — the laughter of 28 girls filled the room, they shared their stories and problems to help calm the anxiety of leaving the loving arms of Chicuchas Wasi. The girls are ready; they will take their eight years of CW preparation with them to their new public high school. The girls shared a warm homecoming type alumnae meeting and the girls look forward to having more of this familiar and trusted connection to the CW family they will miss.

Our relationship with the CW 58 Alumnae is very trusted, and since many girls are harassed by stressed-out parents and some are forced out of school due to the economic struggle their families suffer. Our connection to the girls has enabled us to know of their progress and struggles, and we have often matched them up with donations from kind people who visit our school to help them stay in school, pay for their uniforms, books and supplies and fees at the public high school. We remain the touchstone for these girls.

CHAPTER 24

Visitor Testimony

Children look to adults to care for them, and then they become our teachers." —Rae

"As a Peruvian born educator familiar with Peruvian culture, and Latin American viewpoints, I can confirm that Chicuchas Wasi is a rare asset that has successfully built, from the curriculum to the bricks, a school for female children that truly responds to the century-old social and economic imbalance these children suffer, constructing, with a mountain of dedication, a new horizon. Through education much can be accomplished, but it is the educator who is the first-line worker in this fight for justice and equality. Chicuchas Wasi is an organization that deserves a greater level of long-term support in order to train a new generation of female teachers and leaders, and ultimately raise and educate female children who can be self-sufficient and knowledgeable of their human rights." – Dr. Luis Kong, CSU, Sacramento, CA.

Five-Year-Old Student and Her Father address Graduation Day

The graduating 6th grade students had an emotional closing ceremony for Chicuchas Wasi School year 2015; the school Mayor held the Peruvian flag for the last time. This was a bittersweet moment for all those saying goodbye to their beloved school. The changing of the guard ceremony to install the new 2016 CW school Mayor was when the outgoing mayor placed the banner over the head and onto the incoming mayor and completing the transfer of responsibility.

At the start of our 2015 school closing ceremony, there was an unusual event that took place that Ruth shared with me. If you ever wonder if CW is making a difference in the lives of those less fortunate, this story will move you.

The final day of school arrived and the closing ceremony program was ready to begin when a five-year-old kindergarten student approached one of the teachers to ask if she could please tell her poem. Director Ruth Uribe smiled and nodded yes. Our little student recited her poem that she created in memory since she does not read or write yet. She told of her love for her school and her professor Ruth and that she was very sad she had to leave. She said no other school would love her like CW or hug her like everyone does at CW or listen to her like they do at her precious school. She was choked up but managed to finish her poem. Director Ruth was deeply moved and then the father came up to her and told her he found a job in the jungle and they had to move. He wanted to thank her for all the help CW had given to his family and they are more united now because of CW parent groups and they know they will not find another school like CW, but their daughter WILL go to school. They understand now that her education is important. "Muchas Gracias," he told Ruth, with tears running down his face. Ruth was crying, and I am sure the audience was too.

Chicuchas Wasi Alumnae Girls — SHINE.

Every December since 2013, when we filled all grades in our new CW school, we have graduated from 10 to 11 students onto public high school. CW created the CW Alumnae Sisterhood in 2014 to be able to mentor and support our graduates in high school; they meet semi-monthly to share progress, tell stories and problems and offer guidance to the next graduating class.

When Flor came to Chicuchas Wasi School, she spoke only her mother language, Quechua. She is a child so smart that she could not only learn to read and write in Spanish to become an excellent student and woman, she also taught us to love our mother language, Quechua, even more. She had to learn all of this while also learning Spanish to be able to communicate with her fellow students and continue her studies. Flor is a young woman, brave and very prepared to confront the challenge of secondary school in the city. I know she will succeed because she is well prepared, intellectually and emotionally. She was in the first graduation class of in 2013.

Ruth tells me: *"Flor came to Cusco with her mother from the rural countryside speaking only Quechua. Every door was closed to them and she and her mother had to overcome all they lacked personally for city life, having lived in rural simplicity. They could not find a school to accept Flor until they came to Chicuchas Wasi where she was given an education in values, a quality academic education including Spanish and personal empowerment. We prepared her to confront her difficulties and dream of a better future knowing that she could reach her goals, in spite of the added difficulty of caring for a sick mother and their extreme poverty. Since her graduation three years ago, she has held the 1st place in achievements in her public high school. Flor dreams of becoming a psychologist so she can help those who need it, and especially her mother who found life's struggle so overwhelming that alcohol took over her life; young Flor has one more difficulty to overcome. CW team stands by her and she will reach her dream."*

Chicuchas Wasi is able to educate and empower 125-130 girls each year and our girls are changing their families and communities by their example, even teaching parents how to use their voice and to vote. YOU have believed in them and your faith in them has fueled them forward. Just look our girls. CW is truly their home away from home.

Health Issues from Summer Malnutrition at Home

At the start of every school year in March, the City provides a medical team consisting of an MD and a Nurse to evaluate each girl's health status during the March school physical of all our schoolgirls, including lab work. Summer vacation at home also means there will be no nutritious school meals until March. Money is scarce, and often so is food at home; our girls frequently return malnourished with new health issues like severe anemia and Tuberculosis.

The Growth and Development of children is as important as the Education of Girls and serious business at CW. With good nutrition from our meal program (oatmeal breakfast and high protein lunch), CW has improved the health of our girls (thanks to our great cooks) and the added vitamins and iron. This is one more serious health issue often found in the girls we serve.

Summer is Over

Everywhere summer vacation is anticipated as a fun time for school children, and Cusco children are no different. In Cusco, summer school break is from December to March each year and gives everyone a welcome rest. However, for the staff there are some things best done during this quiet time that cannot easily be dealt with during the busy school year.

Classroom and bathroom maintenance are some of those chores undertaken during this time when the school is otherwise closed. With only two weeks left until the start of school, our dedicated teachers decided to paint their classrooms in bright new colors — peach, lime, cream, orange, etc. — to give a fresh new look to start the year. They showed up ready to paint their classrooms with their own vacationing children in tow. This is yet another example of our incredible CW team and their enthusiastic spirit that filled the last days of Cusco summer with cheerful positive energy ready to begin again on March third. Our teachers are well prepared educators and our students are the winners.

On the first day of school, the returning students line up for the assembly on the patio grounds and show the incoming kindergarten four- and five-year-olds the ropes. In January, the teachers complete the curriculum work and all subjects are prepared and ready; the updated text/workbooks are waiting piled up in every classroom. Classroom walls are bright and cheerful to dazzle the incoming students returning in their freshly laundered uniforms and they hug their classmates as deep bonds are reunited and all make ready for the year.

The Peruvian Ministry of Education arrives the first week to introduce a few new additions to the curriculum they are requiring of all schools.

The cooks are busy with shopping, carrying the big sacks of rice, lentils, and other food items to the school, crossing several fields from the main road with the help of some of the teachers and then preparing the first nutritious hot meal of the year.

Life is never dull at the CW School and spirits run high with enthusiasm no matter the challenges. Such is the way of life in Cusco.

The School Van Saga

CW School urgently needed a school van to pick up and deliver our little ones to and from school safely daily. It was so urgent that without it the younger ones didn't come regularly because parents could not pay for the public bus or go with the little ones. Rain brought mud. Hail hurt your head. Hot sun burned you. Or maybe you got tired if you walked to much and wandered off somewhere else. Then there were other issues about little girls walking or riding public buses and the predators who waited for them.

We found the funds (pleading to our families and friends) and bought the van. We assigned a teacher to wait at each pickup van stop and accompany the girls to school. We had pickup points at three different locations for the three trips each way our driver made every day. If you have ever been to our school on the unpaved road you must use to get there, you can imagine the beating the van took with three round trips a day, for the entire school year from 2014 to 2016. When it rains hard like it does in Cusco, the roads become a mess and the van would just slide around instead of going forward, and the downhill road to the school dropped off to a ravine on one side and so might the van.

Our tired school van needed a replacement as soon as possible for a larger, stronger school bus. We have had so many breakdowns and even had to rent a van to deliver girls back to their home drop-off area at times, so this was now urgent.

Then one day, during summer vacation, Ruth called to tell me that the driver took the van to service it before school and on the way to the service center the side slider door just flew off — seriously slid back and flew off. No one was in the van besides the driver, thank God. I could only imagine all the girls jammed in the van flying out the opening after the door. It was repaired with a new door and firmly secured in time for school, but we were killing this van with our use and the roads. Both Ruth and I went to work to get a real school bus.

I was on a mission to get a real school bus and get it soon. Soon took about a year, as the cost was an outrageous $65,000 Mercedes bus in Peru and the cheapest we could find. In the end we bought it and we all breathed a little easier. There was one less round-trip as well for the driver.

Bilingual Young Women
Will Always Find Work in Cusco!

Cusco is the historic home of the well-known Inca Empire, Machu Picchu, and popular tourist attractions known worldwide today. Young people who can speak English will always find work in many areas of Cusco's tourist industry. Frequently, travelers come to visit our school, and in 2014 a tourist named Pamela came to learn about our Chicuchas Wasi (CW) School for rural Girls. She was so taken by our schoolgirls, their passion to learn and the charm of our 112 girls that she suggested and sponsored our first English class that continues today.

Pamela's keen eye took in the broad focus of CW's many programs and the unique educational style of the school. We teach values like *Honesty, Generosity, Respect,* etc., a value posted over each classroom door, and take pride in the teacher/student relationships and bonding, the open affection of our students, and their enthusiasm for their education. She saw the value of adding English to prepare them for more future job options and acted. Thank You, Pamela.

CHAPTER **25**

San Pedro Market

"Education is the key out of poverty,
But children hold the key to our hearts." —Rae

A QUICK TRIP with Ruth to my favorite Cusco market to shop for quinoa, veggies and bread is colorful eye candy to me. A lined brown face with thick black braids that fall to her waist is tied together with yarn at the end. She sits unstressed on top of her practical soft cushion of woven mantas, her full brown breasts hang freely, the nipples still pressed flat and waiting for her tiny bundle wrapped tightly in a blanket and tied with a colorful woven cord. Her little one of about three months is distracted by the two three-year-olds playing next to her and has momentarily let go of her comfort; white drops slide off the left side of her pink mouth. She remembers, and cries rooting for the warm comfort, grabs hold, and greedy slurping sounds silence the whimpers. Not even teenage boys bother to look at the exposed round breast, with babies attached like dots on fabric. No one notices a naked breast, and they are everywhere, available to pacify an upset child. Occasionally the face attached to the breast shows years of life well past making milk, but available just the same. Again no one notices.

The train arrives in the middle of Cusco's San Pedro Market. The market spreads out up and down side streets and connects to its over-flowing enclosed center. Vendors under blue plastic stretched on poles sell olives in barrels, dried raisons and fresh-smelling brown bread and corn flour bread. Buses, cars, pedestrians and shoppers push and shove their way through. Hungry dogs scavenge and strike gold often and can be seen running out of the main building with a hunk of dripping red meat clutched between bared teeth, with an angry Indian woman in full layered skirts in chase, shouting in Quechua and swinging her fists at the dog. The savvy dog dives into a narrow path and gets away. The woman's face is screwed up with her frustration; resigned, she turns to go inside to her booth.

CW Girls Find Their Voice and Their Vote

After years of gender inequality in every area of life in Cusco, indigenous rural women still believe they are inferior to men and have "neither voice nor vote." And this message is passed down to their daughters who believe it is true and are destined to suffer in life. The rural women, and the mothers and grandmothers of our girls, believe they have no power to make decisions to change the gender inequality that keeps them impoverished and silent. Ruth decided CW School would teach the girls to vote.

To provide our girls with greater understanding, CW School Director, Ruth, started an annual CW school election to elect a school Mayor. Every class nominated a candidate, and the class had to help their candidate prepare for the upcoming big debate with the eight other candidates (one from each of the eight classrooms). A moderator was chosen to keep order and monitor the time allocated for each candidate to speak. The stage was set like an actual election debate, with the setting and props CW borrowed from the local government organization that oversees elections. The debate was presented to all 120 students at the time. They were to listen, learn and think about the candidate so they might make a good choice for school Mayor.

Secret ballots were filled out and our Mayor was chosen. Every girl is finding her voice and how to use it, and now our students will know how and why they must vote to bring equality to all indigenous women and girls of Cusco. This is one way we are changing the futures of poor indigenous girls little by little.

The girls are expected to teach their mothers and fathers how to vote and the importance for them to do so.

CHAPTER 26

Our Alumnae Girls
Ask for Help — 2017

"Children are born with pure loving hearts,
but must learn that they are wonderful, intelligent,
talented and much loved by adults." —Rae

CHICUCHAS WASI (CW) School has had many successes during our 20 years dedicated to the education of poor indigenous girls who are finally able to go to school. But the socioeconomic level in which they live has not changed and is not something CW school can change.

During the last two months, the Peruvian public schools (not CW) have been on strike and left our high school girls in limbo. Their families pushed them harder to work and as the strike continued the risk that they would not return to school grew. The strike finally ended, but now there is additional pressure on the high school girls by the Peruvian Ministry of Education to make up the lost school time during the strike adding more stress and a greater level of desperation that the girls must struggle with. They desperately want to stay in school, but the family wants them to work.

Alone, emotional, depressed and confused, they suffered quietly. A CW 2013 graduate and exceptional high school student in her 4th year of high school died at 15 years of age suddenly last week. Her friends rushed to their beloved CW to tell Director Ruth how she struggled at home with her 'auntie' (non-relative tia) and that they came to see Ruth for comfort and support.

At a recent CW Alumni Sisterhood meeting, our now 12- to 15-year-old girls will graduate in public high school and speak openly about the difficult reality they face every day at home. Like our 120 younger girls at the CW Primary School for Girls, the high school girls confront a list of serious challenges: absolute poverty, malnutrition due to inadequate nutrition at home, poor health, family dysfunction, alcoholism and abuse, neglect and abandonment, to name a few. Those with loving and supportive parents represent approximately 30-40% of all parents. Some of our girls abandoned by both parents end up with a 'Tia' (a non-relative and unloving caretaker) who uses and abuses them. The CW staff tries and generally is successful in keeping them in school and letting them know they are loved and being empowered for their future. In addition to academic education, CW is about LOVE and nurturing these young girls. We provide a nutritious daily meal, and our girls' health is improved. Healing their hearts will be ongoing and our staff is dedicated to filling our girls with the love that is often absent at home. We are blessed with success and strong confident girls when they move onto high school, but they now struggle alone away from the loving arms of CW and are asking CW for the emotional support all young girls need. The CW Alumnae Sisterhood has been ongoing and in constant contact with the older girls to mentor and assist them with money to buy their high school supplies and uniforms when needed.

Later our CW Alumnae girls reached out to us, saying their challenges have become too difficult for them alone and asked for immediate psychological help.

During this crisis, Ruth reported that the girls tell us they have no one. She reports that when listening to their stories and troubles, she asked them what it was they needed most and was most urgent. They answered: *"We need a Psychologist's help, and to know that we are still part of CW emotionally. When we were students here in CW school, we knew we could trust you, that you listened to us and protected us, and you gave us the strength we needed — now we feel alone."* Ruth added that one girl told her: *"I have a mama with alcohol problems. She becomes very sad when I tell her something because she doesn't understand me and is not able to advise me, so I have to make all the decisions alone. She is very timid and afraid, so I have to protect her, but I need help from someone I can tell my problems to who will advise me and help me to see what I cannot see."*

After an emotional few days confronting their reality and listening to the stories of the Alumnae girls, we understand they cannot manage alone, and CW must remain their safety net. We must create a formal program for our still very young girls who have gone onto high school, to help them continue their education and prepare them for a bright and sunny future.

The 'Bernadette' Program was Created

1- Ongoing psychological guidance with the school psychologist.

2- Emotional support and affection from CW teachers and admin staff.

3- Search for a social worker to identify the socioeconomic needs at home.

4- Financial help for high school registration in March for 50% of the girls to pay for the public high school registration fees, uniforms and supplies.

5- The high school girls want to be big sisters and will give talks to the 5th and 6th grade girls about what they are living through and how they must defend themselves by preparing themselves for what they will experience when they leave CW school.

6- Formal committed monthly meetings in addition to personal or group meetings and conversations with CW when needed.

CW Will Have 58 Alumnae in 2019 Who Will Need Us

At the end of 2017, Chicuchas Wasi School for Girls was abruptly alerted of the death of a 15-year-old alumna, and the reality that our 36 CW Alumnae girls attending public high school were ALL experiencing serious emotional stress and parental pressure to quit school and earn money for the family. Some told us they suffered physical abuse and felt very alone without the immediate go-to CW support and mentoring they received before they graduated. They came to us in mass asking for help and to become part of CW in a deeper way — specifically they asked for a psychologist's help. We mobilized immediately and created a new program to address these issues.

Dr. Alejandro is a wonderful and sensitive psychologist who joined our team and created the 'Bernadette Program' for our Alumnae that has proven very effective. We are also working more with the CW girls and parents to better prepare them for the issues the older girls have revealed. For more than 20 years working to bring gender equality in education to underserved girls, we have learned this is an especially slow process with an undereducated and poor rural population with severe dysfunction in their domestic lives. He meets every Thursday after school in his home with the Alumnae girls first for a snack. They then present and discuss the most pressing problems they are facing.

Dr. Alejandro has come up with several small business ideas to relieve the financial pressure on them to contribute to the family economy and still stay in school. The girls have learned to make fabric dolls to sell while discussing smaller issues as they work. A volunteer pastry chef is teaching the girls to make cakes and cookies to sell, and with the sale of the cakes and their hand-made dolls they

JUMP ON THE LOVE TRAIN

will be able to earn some money to help pay for high school and help their families.

The domestic dysfunction is covered in weekly/monthly meetings with parents and more often with the girls in small groups or individually as needed. Dr. Alejandro has given each girl his private cell number and is on call 24/7 for them in an emergency.

The new school year added 10 new graduates and totaling 46 Alumnae girls in the Bernadette Program. The CW primary school girls are also benefiting from Dr. Alejandro's work with the high school girls, and better able to prepare the younger girls for future hurdles in public high school. We will soon have to split the growing Alumnae group into smaller groups to be able to give voice to each girl.

Our younger CW schoolgirls also have their time with Dr. Alejandro to confront their family problems and to prepare them in advance of graduation for the reality of public school. He meets with the parents of the CW girls monthly or more often if needed to address any issues that come up in one-on-one private meetings or group talks with the students. He is on-call to address any urgent problem that Director Ruth is concerned about.

Dr. Alejandro's various programs (for the primary school girls, the Alumnae girls and both sets of parents) has made a huge difference in the school, for staff, parents and especially for the girls. Our girls have been able to open up to each other and to Dr. Alejandro about any serious problems and they are being addressed by him with the parents. The student bond and support for one another and CW staff continues to grow stronger.

The Importance of Teaching a Marketable Skill to Our School Girls

The experience of working with our former students has taught us that when students leave the CW free school and enter the public high school, our alumnae are overwhelmed with many fees they cannot pay. The Peruvian Ministry of Education says that education in Peru is free, but the reality is you need to pay fees to enroll, acquire a uniform and buy educational materials. The economic situation their parents face often cannot afford these expenses.

The school was blessed with a donation from Martin Curry, Scotland to purchase a commercial oven, to create a CW Bake School and teach all of our girls from 3rd grade up and the Alumnae girls a productive skill. They can now learn how to bake cakes and cookies to sell for money for school.

This is practical knowledge that our students are learning to be able to continue their journey through high school and beyond. This knowledge will grow each year throughout the school career and is very different from the experience of being a student at the primary school level. The bake school is fully implemented with tools and pans, a mixer, etc., and will not require much of a budget or a separate location. They are being taught to create a budget, shopping list, and keep a record of sales to see if they are really earning money. Money management for baking flour and spices is being taught also, and will require little money, and the location is at the school at no cost to the students. This skill will give girls the opportunity to earn money to support their studies. This small business was easily put in place at the school, and the support it will provide could eliminate the stress of financial hardship around school fees and help them achieve their goal to achieve a career.

CHAPTER 27

Not All Girls Have the Same Preparedness for School

"The greatest gift a person can give a child is love."
—Rae

MOST GIRLS WHO enroll each March are eager to go to school and are prepared to some extent with some social experience and manners. However, we also receive girls who need our special attention to be able to develop a quality life integrated into society and not be lost forever to isolation. Luz's teacher tells her story.

Luz arrived at our CW educational institution accompanied by her mother in 2017 in hopes of a vacancy. According to the report from the mother, no public school would accept her because of her 'condition' and she was two years behind by then. Since no other school accepted her in the Peruvian Education Ministry system, Luz was accepted by CW School (free of cost) for first grade in 2017 at eight years of age to avoid losing another year of study. The Mother's health was delicate due to a brain tumor and she was sent to Lima to be treated, and for this reason Luz lost two years of study. Thank God her mother now is receiving treatment.

Luz came to Chicuchas Wasi in a situation of complete moral

abandonment; she had aggressive and intolerant behavior with her peers; she was given a psychological learning evaluation that showed a "moderate" intellectual deficit.

For 2018 and after constant requests, she was promoted to second grade over a period of time. Luz worked on her behavior and improved her character with her classmates.

Today Luz is a girl who is very dear to her classmates and is part of the group. All the difficulties that she presented with are changed — she is different: she is very communicative, she shares many things with her companions, she helps her companions, she lends her supplies to the *compañeras* (other girls) who forget to bring theirs, and she is a collaborator in the groups. Luz likes to sing, dance and tell stories and she likes to dress up as a princess. She enjoys her moments in school.

"Luz has difficulty in writing, but not painting because her drawings are very beautiful, but she relates it to her family." —*A Teacher*

Our Mothers Are Hands-On At Our School!

And they work hard on school projects to help their daughters succeed in school. The heavy February and March rains of Cusco have made it impossible for our new bus to traverse the road all the way to the school. The girls must walk across muddy, slippery clay dirt and arrive to school with wet muddy shoes that make the girls and classrooms a mess. Thanks to our California clothes drive, we have a clean clothing change if needed. Also, Ruth found a way to dry off those wet feet, replacing mud caked shoes with classroom slippers their mothers are making out of recycled clothes and sole inserts Ruth learned how to make for inside the classroom use. This has resulted in a cleaner working environment in the classroom. It might seem unimportant to us in developed countries, but not in rural Cusco schools. Imagine thick mud-caked fingers, then on papers, and the blackboard... all a reality without a creative idea like this one. Now at print time Ruth finally convinced the city to bring heavy equipment out once again to grade the road, at least to avoid having a busload of girls slip and slide or worse in this soft clay.

The indigenous culture of this region is not normally outspoken or too talkative; they demonstrate by their actions their enthusiasm and support to educate their girls, an education that they and their mothers never had the opportunity to receive. They work tirelessly at the school in projects like this one, as classroom mothers, and planting and harvesting our vegetable garden to help manage the meal budget. Every year we see more and more mothers and a few more fathers jump in to help their daughter's school.

Our moms and available dads come to harvest the potatoes they plant each year. In 2018 we had a huge harvest, double the quantity of earlier years. Corn, Quinoa, cabbage and lima beans are also planted at the school.

The food our parents plant and harvest ends up on these plates every day and helps to control our hefty food budget. Since we began the meal program two years ago, there has been a big increase in attention, focus and overall health for our 124 girls. We continue to monitor their health at the start of school in March of the new school year.

These are the ways our mothers and fathers speak out to their friends and communities about the importance of education for their daughters and all girls. They understand that their girls will have a much better life with opportunities never dreamed of and escape their poverty.

CHAPTER **28**

Cooperation and Preparing for Everyday Life

*"My most important back-to-school supply doesn't fit in
a backpack, and it can't be ordered online...
It's empathy"* —Noma Tayangaa

WE TEACH CW girls the value of working together to come up with new ideas they never thought of alone and problem-solve with their classmates for the best outcome. Every primary grade uses this style for some subjects, and the girls have learned the value of collaboration with their classmates for great ideas.

One assignment was to depict daily living (project about life) using math and creative problem-solving for a better solution to a problem, sharing resources and more. The girls must write a report on their assignment, explain their findings and present them to the student body. Younger students often eavesdrop, learn and copy the older girls; they too have big dreams and are eager to learn all they can.

Our girls dive into their assignment and don't mind the younger girls who gather around eager to learn about this lesson too. This is one way for our girls to share their realities, daily responsibilities and difficulties, and come up with better ways to reach their daily goals or help their families. CW girls have big dreams for their futures; becoming teachers, nurses, doctors and running their own business one day and empowering each other as they share their realities and positive attitudes.

To exaggerate a point, Ruth created a plan to help our soon-to-graduate girls understand better the huge responsibility and life-changing reality of having a baby too young. The 6th grade girls were each given two raw eggs to care for as if they were their real babies. They could brag about their babies, adorn them to their liking, but they could not neglect them and must protect them from breaking just like in real life.

The 6th grade girls about to move on to a co-ed high school are vulnerable to become teen mothers and needed a graphic learning experience that the raw eggs provided. Having a baby requires preparation that an 11 to 12-year-old is too young to have and the ability to provide and care for the baby regarding housing, food, washing diapers, medical care if needed and so much more. The raw eggs didn't always get the care needed during this lesson and some broke. The girls got the point.

CW Parents Begin to See a New Future for Their Daughters

Cusco rural parents have believed for generations, that educating a girl is a waste of time and more suited to more intelligent boys. This belief has been in place and has limited the advancement of the girls, mothers and grandmothers who came before our girls for many generations. Lately, we are noticing a change during our yearly March Registration of four- and five-year-olds for CW Kindergarten — a new enthusiasm from mothers who are beginning to seize a new attitude within the Chicuchas Wasi School for Girls community. After 20 years of CW School presence working to bring gender equality in education to underserved girls, our parents are seeing a change in their daughters, and families and are coming together to support their daughters' school.

Parents meet with our psychologist (in group or alone) and the CW director to solve sometimes serious domestic problems and also as parents together to create their own ideas to support the school, born of managing life's obstacles with whatever resources they can find. This supportive process is giving new life to these families and a huge achievement for families of the rural community we serve. The enthusiasm and pride they show in their daughters' achievements is apparent as they attend and participate in the parent classes at the school to learn about responsible parenting and how to better protect their daughters. They ask questions during the psychological meetings and are slowly changing their behavior to improve their domestic life — all improving the girls' abilities to do well academically.

Parents organize simple solutions to solve structural school needs. An example: To block the hot Andean sun beating down on their daughters, they recycled plastic bottles to create shade over the school's main patio — half the size of a football field — to prevent heat stroke while the girls perform theatrical history projects for the entire student body, staff and parents. Parents and students collected hundreds of plastic bottles, washed them out and painted the inside different colors to block the sun. They then strung them together creating a long line to reach across the patio, line by line, to block the sun. This was very creative, effective and only used recycled plastic throwaway bottles — while *Pacha Mama* (Mother Earth) smiles.

Our parents created a school vegetable garden the last few years, taking advantage of the rains to supply the school meal program with many fresh vegetables that grow in the fertile soil of rural Cusco. They planted and then returned to harvest the corn, potatoes, cabbage and other vegetables; parents also built the adobe *Cui* (guinea pig) house for a high protein meat production to combat the anemia in 50% of girls, and manual labor for other projects to benefit their daughters.

These are just a few ways our parents are learning to value their own skills and their growing desire to help their daughters. Our parents' life is absolute poverty without the material things we take for granted, but they have found that they can contribute to their daughters' education by working with the other parents to create needed projects they know how to do, like painting the school over the summer. Another win-win for all. So many people expand who they are and benefit personally from our special school for girls — because of the changes they see in our students, and like their parents, siblings who learn from their sisters, cousins and stories they share with neighbors.

"If we do not work with the mothers and fathers, we will not be successful with their daughters. Parents are showing up to lend a hand to grow food, paint the school, build guinea pig cages and more, plus they attend the parents' meetings with the psychologist. The relationship with their daughters is getting better." —Ruth

CHAPTER **29**

CW Celebrates 30 Years!

"We learn about love through the children." —Rae

AFTER 10 YEARS providing emergency shelter for abandoned children, we realized that we could do more, and to improve the lives of these children we needed to look at the cause of child abandonment and poverty. Poor GIRLS must be educated. CW reorganized in 1997 to provide primary school education for rural indigenous girls. CW provides much more than academic education — annual physical exam and treatment for TB and other health issues at school; we provide nutritious daily meals to combat malnutrition at home, psychologist run groups for students and parents, meditation classes to reduce stress and manage their teen emotions, dental care, English instruction, educational field trips and more. Our girls have had opportunities their mothers never dreamed of and will be able to survive economically and provide for their children if needed. CW has come a long way and so have Ruth Uribe (school Administrator) and I (Business Administrator now) over our 30 years working together. Our loyal and hardworking CA board members all bring talents that have made CW successful over the years, and we include our fabulous teachers over the years. We are an amazing team — all of us together.

This would not be a celebration if we could not share our success, happiness and the love that fills us all, here in California and in Cusco with the staff and GIRLS of our Chicuchas WASI SCHOOL for GIRLS – *WITH YOU!*

Chicuchas Wasi is based on *Three Pillars*:

Love, Respect and Dignity

We hold these values dear and expect all employees, teachers and students to learn, teach, practice and embody these values to make a lasting difference and have a quality life. Most people seldom discuss these values. Above every classroom door there is a plaque with a different Value written on it — each class must focus on their Value for that school year.

CW Values used are:

Love, Respect, Dignity, Punctuality, Honesty, Solidarity, Loyalty, Compassion,

and others are added each year.

Each grade must focus on their class Value for the school year, creating examples that they will share with the rest of the student body. In addition, each class will have one month during the year where they demonstrate to the student body their particular class Value through role-play, poems and stories, and sharing how to include this Value in their daily life.

Take 'Respect' for example. When you consistently treat others with respect, the result is they will begin to return that 'Respect' to you. CW school has had the ability to influence 150 girls for eight years. At the end of those eight years, our girls will have been fully exposed to the importance of Values and aware of how they have grown into a better human being, with a dignity that has become a part of who they are and how they act in the world.

At CW school we strive to empower girls to become future leaders and to instill in each girl a comfortable relationship with these Values so that their example will naturally spread to others. Our girls will develop the awareness that they are quality individuals making a difference in their society and the world. Imagine what our girls will bring to the world.

When you do what you love, and love what you do, it doesn't seem like work and time flies. It is hard to believe that Chicuchas Wasi (CW) just completed its 30th year serving the children in need in Cusco, Peru. Chicuchas Wasi students, teachers and staff are all passionate and proud about the incredible impact we have been able to make in the community we serve.

The Chicuchas Wasi success for over 30 years (20 years as a school) for the 123 girls and families we serve is visible through their achievements. Our girls who have gone on to high school have been noticed and many have been honored as the highest achievers at the new high school. These are the same schools that earlier believed our girls did not have the smarts for high school. Just watch them soar, now that they are given the opportunity.

Our fabulous teachers created the entire CW anniversary celebration. Each teacher prepared a presentation with her grade students — the dances, poems, songs, and skits they presented were outstanding.

Where did the years go? When we look at our beautiful school full of red-clad girls of all sizes, we realize that we have accomplished so much for the girls we serve. I have just returned from Cusco where I shared this celebration with Ruth, 123 girls, and the entire CW team. The excitement was high, the music loud, and colorful costumes represented the many villages of the Andes. The girls danced, sang and shared their poems with so much love for their Chicuchas Wasi School. It was palpable, and we were all full to the brim. Ruth and I looked at each other knowingly and passed the tissue. I am speechless to know how to express the blessings that have been bestowed on our small project that began in 1987, and which is not so small anymore.

So, again, I have to bow to you, our faithful supporters, who care about our impact on this community to benefit girls' education. You never abandoned us even during those financially tough years. You know who you are, and you came through.

Blessings to you.

We have loved and found so much joy in our work with the children of Cusco that 30 years have just flown by and we are now planning for the next 30 years.

We plan to keep planning the next year, and the next year after that. Each school year begins in March in the southern hemisphere. During February our teachers receive special training that we provide and that the Ministry of Education offers. Annual maintenance to the school is completed. The parent & daughter interviews began for the next school year enrollment. Selecting the most in need narrows the list immediately as the families with financial means have the public schools where they can send their daughters. School began every March with 15 students per class with a total maximal enrollment of 150.

If you have wondered if we have a plan for self-sufficiency for longevity – WE DO! That will be in the follow up book... in 2020.

A Beneficiary of Chicuchas Wasi has this to Say:

"I have first-hand experience about this amazing organization. I was one of the first children who lived in Chicuchas Wasi 30 years ago when it was founded by Rae Lewis. When I was seven years old, both of my parents passed away leaving my five siblings and I orphaned. It was through a social worker that I met Rae, who took my siblings and I into her home. At that time Chicuchas Wasi was a children's home, where I lived for seven years.

It was through this organization that I received a scholarship to further my studies in the USA. I left Chicuchas Wasi Peru when I was 14 years old, but I was still part of this organization until I graduated from college and became independent.

It was because of CW that today I am a Registered Nurse and I am able to help my family in Peru financially. Today, I travel to Peru once a year to visit family and the school and the rest of the CW family.

Words alone cannot explain how grateful I am for having met Rae Lewis and for giving me not only a place to live, but an education that will last me for a lifetime. Coming from a place where women are still the minority and have fewer opportunities, an education is the foundation to a better life and opportunities in many ways."

There are so many memories that come to mind when I try to remember my childhood in Chicuchas. Sometimes, I take my usual walk around my neighborhood with my dog, and now my son, Julien, and have to pause and imagine how my life would be if my birth parents were still alive and therefore never have met Rae Lewis. It's hard to imagine this life if those events hadn't occurred.

There's no doubt that I feel blessed for this life I was given. I was chosen because she believed in me. I will always be grateful for it and this life and have an appreciation of what life is and can be when you give an opportunity to an individual who perhaps only imagined life out of poverty.

There is probably not much else left to say about CW that hasn't already been said in this book. Over the years, CW meant family and love to me. It brought so many memories, some happy and some sad ones, but at the end it was always good. Sometimes, my older siblings and I would reminisce sharing old stories and memories growing up in CW. It was always a bittersweet feeling to relive those memories.

Today all of us, the initial CW kids, are all grow up and most of us have our own families and have moved on with our own lives and some are still part of the current CW project and involved. We feel lucky and blessed to be the ones who have accomplished many things with our lives and yet also wish everyone deserved opportunities in life and live to their potential."

Rosa Lewis — 30-year member of the CW Family and two-year Board Member

Acknowledgements

Since 1987 when Chicuchas Wasi was founded, the number of generous people who felt called to jump in and help Chicuchas Wasi become the success it is today is so amazing and beyond my wildest expectations it would be impossible to name them all. With all my heart, I am grateful to you all, and you know who you are, for giving so much to raise the standard of living for the children we serve. If your name is not mentioned on these pages, please know how much your love and willing hands have meant to us all.

Leading the pack were the original big-hearted and talented supporters who made an enormous leap of faith when they jumped on the train with me. We had no money, no experience, but lots of love, trust and faith that we could make a difference. I honor our incredible founding members of the Chicuchas Wasi board of directors: Iris Rasmusen — offered her home, Karen Amoruso — CPA extraordinaire, Terry McDonald — Artisan Graphics (extremely talented Graphic Designer), Jon Lopez — Champion Fundraiser, Rae Lewis — Founder of CW, Mary Salfi — T-Shirt sales management and much more. Many of you stayed years, some more than 25 years on the board, holding it all together and together we learned, worked hard and expanded our success.

Selina Galick hauled me to the airport with her truck loaded with big boxes of donations for the CW Shelter on almost every trip from California to Cusco over the early years. Director, Roger Pacheco of the San Francisco Bay Area Varig Airline Co., allowed me to take them (all overweight) free of charge to Peru. Betty Woods and Earl Herr made countless visits to Cusco, helped haul supplies and help in any way they could.

Philip Voysey of Australia returned to Cusco in 1987 to help me get the shelter up and running and was enormous moral and physical support — we both learned step-by-step with each passing day about the Peruvian red tape through which we had to dance.

My ex-pat friend of the Rumichaka Village, Beverly Elder, gave me her love, a quiet space in her rural home, a sanctuary to recharge me and prevent burnout as needed. Lynn Woolsey assisted CW with visitor visas to bring CW staff to California.

My childhood friend, Susan Dupuis (Flying Fingers Secretarial and Copy Center), helped with original newsletters, printing and editing documents at our startup, and together with Kathy Bardea sold many pieces of Peruvian jewelry in their office. Sue is the talented editor with the eagle eye on my first book.

Always grassroots, we held and still offer many fundraisers: Christmas sales of Peruvian crafts, an outstanding Andean Concert with Colectivo Anqari and Chaskinakuy with many generous donations of talent and time. Student Itzel Macedona recruited and led high school volunteers for the concert and to help on many projects. Sonoma merchants generously donated to our CW Auction and many more lent a hand in so many ways. To the concert MC goes much appreciation to Luis Kong and his MC talent and theatrics with the kids in Urubamba during a visit.

Packing and sorting donated medicines with Lynn Harris, Betty Woods, Linda Schill, and so many more who jumped in to help during CW events here and there in the 30 years. Tesa Carlson protected and managed my personal finances the first years. Di Webster and Jan Case provided mentorship in building CW bylaws and a CW business plan. Jen Ward let me share her beautiful photography. Thanks to the Index Tribune and Sonoma Sun newspapers for the great stories about CW since the beginning. Val Robichaud, Editor of Sonoma Sun, has provided great press coverage for special events over the last 15 years.

Jerry Shover delivered to Urubamba many large boxes of needed kitchen supplies for our new B&B in Urubamba. Chela Alca lent her able hands to jump in and help in Cusco and Urubamba here and there. Michael Catanzaro — Fabulous and generous Sonoma Web Designer for creating our beautiful CW website. Jim Whitous — CaféMac, Apple guru and ever-available consult for my computer headaches. Manuel Villacorta, MS, RD from SF, provided nutritional guidance and created special online fundraisers for the CW Meal Program.

Santa Rosa Middle School teacher Carol Kovatch created and continues with several fundraisers for CW School in the midst of the Sonoma fires where she lost her own home. Stuart Veitch — Director of the Chicuchas Wasi UK group — continues to offer funding support as well as much appreciated emotional support and advice. Julianna Anderson — my early writing practice partner. Monica Arguelles, pastry chef, donated hours of food preparation for fundraising events. Steve Burdick — very active board member for a time. Pat and Norm Brown provided much love and ready hands. Zoila Calvo Perez, owner of Fresca Peruvian Restaurant, created fundraisers in San Francisco. Jose Nararro, owner of Sazon Peruvian Restaurant, held fundraisers in Santa Rosa and created fundraisers for CW. Earline Reid, US Embassy in Lima, gave Rosa her life-changing student visa in Lima in 1994. Jeanette Rosazza, Café Hailey in Cusco, opened her home to me, Phil and our first CW child, Ronald, while we got started. Noel and Maureen Schmidt were wonderful host parents for Rosa in California when she was a foreign exchange student at Ursuline High School. Carol Dickason, Graphic Designer, helped when I was stuck and was one who never said no. Jim Plunkett, President of Peruvian American Chamber of Commerce, opened so many doors for donations in Peru and organized the AM-CHAM Golf Tournament benefit for CW. Luis Gallindo, lawyer in Lima, provided legal guidance and delivery to certain important meeting. Victor Azpuecuelta, lawyer in Cusco, created the legal document for CW as a non-profit in Peru and more. Erik Vera, lawyer and CW staunch supporter who happens to be Ruth's husband, is always on stand-by to lend a hand.

Thank you for your generous offer to read my manuscript before it goes to print, your comments are most valuable; thanks to Andy Weinberger, Margaret Noel, Noreen Schumann, Leonard Pieraccini. The original travel fundraising idea came from Aurelio Aguirre and his travel company; thank you for teaching me how to do our first CW Andean Adventure as a fundraiser for CW. Thank you Gina Giles for the beautiful mural of the children you painted on the dining room wall of the Cusco house.

For about 20 years we held many folk art fundraisers, earring sales and clothing drives at St. Leo's Church and great appreciation goes to the late Msg. Jack O'Hare who never said no. So many volunteers over the years jumped in to help with whatever was needed — enough to fill another book. Your support made all the difference.

For about 25 years, Gregg Stubbs, SF lawyer who was introduced to me by Msg. Jack O'Hare has provided personal and CW necessary legal support and guidance when needed and I am grateful. Muchas Gracias, Gregg. Marilu Zubiri and I met over a three-hour cup of coffee about four years ago, and she has jumped on the train to translate this book into Spanish for the Peru community. Mil gracias, Marilu.

Two special men hold a place in my heart: my son, Lenny Pieraccini, who came to visit his mom many times because she missed him (and he missed me too), and often lent a hand in the CW Shelter in Urubamba with the shelter kids. He was young and a big hit with the kids, plus he could drive the 4x4 on the terrible roads and the kids loved it when he (not me) took them fishing. Muchas Gracias, hijo mio.

My CW Peruvian son, Efrain Valles M., has been a CW family member since 1990. Efrain grew up in CW and as an adult has become an active board member, a father of three and an amazing ambassador for the CW school today. I doubt we would have survived a few very difficult periods without his loyal ambassadorship that brought so many people to the school from many countries and who subsequently became financial CW supporters and still are today. He has provided a Christmas Party for the school and so much more. Thank you, Efrain, for your big heart and dedication to the CW school.

Today we have our incredible California CW board team, and we manage the fundraising and legal status of our non-profit in the states. The fabulous board members today: Isabel Craft — Treasurer, Mary Salfi, Betty Woods — Secretary, Rae Lewis — President, and Rosa Lewis who, like Efrain, also grew up in CW and came to CA on scholarship in 1994.

Most important to the success of Chicuchas Wasi has been the contribution of Ruth Uribe Barrios, born, raised and educated in Cusco and who understood her culture well and how to make a lasting difference for the children we serve. In spite of the resistance from her parents, she left her government teaching position to join me in the CW Shelter and soon demonstrated her leadership. We became co-leaders and she eventually created the special CW School for Girls we have today for long lasting societal change for gender equality in education. Without Ruth's academic skill mixed with her passion to make a difference for the children, the school success today would only be a dream. Together we make the perfect team, each with needed skills, perseverance, and faith in the hand that guides us for the success we have achieved.

Most important today is our invaluable CW SCHOOL STAFF:

- Simeon — CW Chauffeur and all-round handy man at the school
- Chief Cook — Sayda
- Margareta — Assistant Cook
- Yony — School Secretary
- Dr. Alejandro — Psychologist

Gratitude to our dedicated TEACHERS:

- Ruth Uribe Barrios — School Administrator and Director
- Gloria Vera — Assistant Director
- Rosita — Kindergarten for 4-year-olds
- Luz — Kindergarten for 5-year-olds
- Pamela — 1st Grade
- Elizabeth — 2nd Grade
- Jessica — 3rd Grade
- Karent Meleni Mendoza Tecsi — 4th Grade
- Haide Lenes Fanola — 5th Grade
- Giovanna Calderon — 6th Grade

What a multitalented and passionate teaching team we have at Chicuchas Wasi School for Girls in Cusco. Thank you for your dedication to our girls.

About the Author

Rae was born in San Francisco and raised in Sausalito, California. She and her husband and three sons later settled in rural Sonoma County. Rae has many skills from a variety of professions: Registered Nurse in several local hospitals, Real Estate Professional, and worked in many aspects of her Family Business as a teenager where she gained many skills that proved useful later running a non-profit.

Later, she moved to Cusco, Peru and founded the Chicuchas Wasi Organization and lived in the CW Shelter project for the next 10 years setting up and building a team for a successful Chicuchas Wasi today.

Eventually it was time to reorganize the nonprofit, in favor of the CW School for Indigenous Girls and turned over the Cusco project to the capable hands of Ruth Uribe, a resident leader in CW since 1994 and creator of the school. Rae returned home to Sonoma to manage the business side of Chicuchas Wasi and continues to do so today, after 31 years. This is a labor of love she says, and not really work.

Chicuchas Wasi

School for Girls
· Cusco, Peru ·

For more information :

www.chicuchaswasi.org
FaceBook : chicuchaswasi
Email: Chicuchas_wasi@sonic.net

CPSIA information can be obtained
at www.ICGtesting.com
Printed in the USA
FSHW022231100519

9 781977 208996